Introduction

Not all Motorcycle adventures need a g
divorce, a small fortune and a bundle o
Motorcycle adventures are there for you to define based on the emotional and physical resources you have available.

I have been motorcycling since I was sixteen and much of that was restricted to day rides out or commuting to work. Now in my fifties I am discovering that the immense enjoyment I get out of riding a bike can be further enhanced by turning a ride into a trip.

Don't wait for that mythical time when you can take three months to ride the America's. Don't focus on that two week trip three years from now. Get out there and have your adventure today.

This book describes how I pushed my boundaries to go a little bit further afield in a short space of time and with it experienced a trip that will remain with me forever. This is one example but as I say define your own. A few years earlier I did a one night trip to the Islay in the Inner Hebrides and camped on the edge of a beach facing the Atlantic. I will never forget that sun set and the warmth I felt in my heart as I sat there alone with only a Laphroaig for company. It was bliss.

The Idea

"You have to talk to my workmate Willie" said Amber "he was talking about a fantastic place for a motorcycle adventure". This was in the summer of 2010 and it took quite a long time before I finally caught up with Willie who happened to live on the same street, to find out where this great biking destination was. Willie has an infectious enthusiasm for motorcycling owning a beat up Honda Dominator, and a lovely old Honda Africa Twin.

The mystery destination was the Nordkapp in Norway, I had never heard of it. It's the most northern point in Europe, 700 miles above the Arctic Circle and 1300 miles from the North Pole. Willie enthusiastically described the long but amazing route up through Norway with fantastic scenery and great wild camping spots. He loaned me a book "Norway's Arctic Highway" by John Douglas to further wet my appetite and encouraged me to join him on a trip.

To be honest after some research I felt as if it was a retirement trip due to the fact there were no longer any ferry links to Norway; getting there and back would take six days alone. Still I was hooked on the idea and continued to mull over my options. Amber encouraged me to find a way to make it happen. "Have your adventures while you're still fit enough to enjoy them" she said.

The most I could take from a holiday allocation point of view was two weeks and two days and although it would be tight I felt sure I could do it within that timeframe. I had made my mind up so I contacted Willie in the autumn of 2011 and said I was up for it. I knew he planned to combine it with a wider trip taking in the Balkans, so I proposed that we spend at least part of our trip together.

As a biking enthusiast since I was sixteen I had been on many trips with the most adventurous taking place during the last few years. These have included a group Triumph tour of Greece, a trip with a Belgian friend Kurt down to the Swiss Alps and a more recent reunion of old friends with a bike trip through Arizona and New Mexico; none of these were on the same scale as the Nordkapp in terms of mileage and time.

The Preparation

Trying to choose a route was difficult as there were pluses and minuses to them all, and I had Willie's preferences to consider. There was the option of a ferry from Harwich to Esbjerg in Denmark but the journey down through England was 470miles. Another interesting choice was a freight ferry from Immingham to Kristiansand which was my preferred choice until I read that it could be unpredictable. With my limited time, a day's delay would be a disaster. I ended up going with the Newcastle to Amsterdam Ferry departing 29th June returning the 16th of July 2012. On the way up I would catch the Hirtshals Denmark to Bergen ferry on the 1st July and start the Norwegian part of my journey from there.

I decided to go ahead and book as Willie is more of a last minute man. I also felt as if it would free him up to do as he pleased i.e. join me part of the way, all of the way or not at all. On the 8th of January 2012 I booked my ferries and with it, I was credit card committed. I booked a hotel in Denmark for the first night on continental Europe roughly 400 miles from Amsterdam. I wanted to have a dry and known destination as it would be a long ride on that first day. From there I would have 200 miles to do in the morning to the next ferry point.

Preparation beyond that was all about reading the Arctic Highway book, looking at web sites and dreaming. The route I would be taking through Norway was predominantly the E6 north. At Mo I Rana the E6 becomes the Arctic Highway also known as the blood road due to the number of World War II Prisoners of war who perished there constructing and upgrading it. The Arctic Highway runs all the way to Kirkines near the Russian border. I would leave it at Karasjok on my route south towards Finland.

My bike was a 2009 BMW R1200GS which was more than capable of doing the trip. I had already added bits and pieces that would all come in useful; luggage, engine protection and a Sat Nav mount. I also had an Airhawk seat to keep my 53 year old bum in reasonable shape. I had camping gear that I used on my annual 'get away from it all' overnighters to the Highlands so I was more or less set, though I did buy a few bits and pieces such as vacuum pack bags, a tent peg mallet and thermal underwear.

I felt a huge sense of excitement about this trip. It felt like an adventure especially as I would be doing some, or maybe all of it, alone. On that point Willie was very quiet and was nowhere to be seen. He was supposed to go on holiday to Australia but that never happened.

He did stop off in late March when he saw me in the in my garden. "I'm definitely still going" he said "I'll book up closer to the time". He talked about leaving earlier than me and meeting me on the Bergen ferry. "OK great" I said not entirely convinced he would be there. The good thing was I would not be relying on him. If he comes great, if he doesn't then thanks for telling me about the route, was exactly how I felt.

On Friday June 1st a mail popped into my inbox from Willie. He was asking for details on when I thought we would reach the Nordkapp so he could arrange his Russian visa. He said he had three weeks off and was booking ferries that weekend with a departure date of 28th June. Maybe Willie is coming after all.

The final weeks were a little tense but exciting as I balanced work commitments against getting away. It seems in my job as an IT Consultant there is never a good time to go, but going I was. I had a request to fly out to Chennai in India a few days before my trip was due to end ; I stood my ground and said I couldn't do it.

I bought some final bits and pieces including some boil in the bag camping meals and received a folding spatula and spice box (my suggestion) for Father's Day. I was organised and ready to ride. When I say organised I was the least organised I ever had been for a two week plus trip. I had one nights hotel booked and had no hard destinations or accommodation between Bergen and the Nordkapp or the Nordkapp and Amsterdam. I had no idea if I would be on my own or if indeed Willie would be in the Ferry boarding queue at Hirtshals. I made a choice to stop reading the Arctic Highway book in advance, and decided I would read about the road ahead each night as I travelled.

On Wednesday the 27th of June two days before departure a further email popped up in my inbox from Willie. He said he was booked and ready to leave tomorrow (one day ahead as planned) but he had a lung infection and was struggling to make it. The next day Willie confirmed he couldn't make it.

One day to go and I was finally clear that this was indeed going to be a solo trip. I felt a mixture of excitement and fear but it had heightened my sense of adventure in making the trip. I would be travelling alone for 5000 miles with no-one but myself to answer to. This was what real adventures were made off. I am comfortable with my own company and have to be in my line of work but to take over two weeks out in a leisure context was a new experience for me. It would be an interesting experiment.

On Thursday the 28th of June I said my goodbyes at work. I was working down south at a client in Swindon and wandered out excitedly to get my taxi. There had been a lot of interest in my trip from those colleagues who had asked where I was off too. The Arctic Circle gets their attention and doing it alone adds to the package. A common reaction was a look of puzzlement/horror/envy followed by the words "What does your wife think?"

This was not only colleagues but friends and family too. My brother half jokingly said "We Mason's go for two weeks holiday with our wife in July." "Not this Mason" I replied proudly. Amber and I have spent a lot of time apart since we first met 13 years ago as my job demands constant travel. The fact that I do this much travel only heightened the level of questioning from others wondering why I would take more time out on my own.

Amber and I have both struggled with my lifestyle at times, but also recognise it has brought many benefits to us as individuals and as a couple. After a tough ending to my first marriage I was vulnerable and lost. I had just gotten into IT Consulting when I met Amber. We both know if I had not been restricted to seeing her every third weekend on my return trips from California, where I was posted, we would not have survived. I would have clung to her for safety, and she would have run away in fear. The lifestyle and the forced independence it brings have taught me to value myself and my own time. That is what this trip is about. I am a very lucky man that I have a wife who not only respects that, but taught me it.

The taxi ride was trouble free and after an hour I arrived at Terminal 5. The Heathrow blues set in as a 30 minute flight delay popped up on the screen. Past experience tells me Heathrow don't do 30 minute delays. I bought my Motorcycle

News and settled in the lounge. We eventually boarded and after a further hour of sitting on the runway we took off. I have an unusual method of counting down to events and that is by x number of flights to go. In this case I had one flight to go and it felt good.

When we arrived at Glasgow I had a message from the taxi driver asking me to call him when I land so he wouldn't get caught too long in the pick-up car park. He didn't leave his number so I called the company to contact him to say I was there. He finally arrived and we had a skirmish over his abrupt assertion his number would be on my phone as a missed call. "Nope" I replied as my phone was switched off in flight. He was adamant that it would and he was beginning to irritate me.

We headed out of the car park and he switched on the radio. Italy was beating Germany 2-0 in the semi final of the European Championship which was a surprise. I looked out at the weather which was cloudy but dry and I hoped that would stay that way and defy the weather forecast which was predicting heavy rain for the following day.

When I arrived home Amber and I drank some red wine and talked about the final preparations for the trip. I asked her to shoot some night before video with the bike and I in the garage. I stood there with a glow describing my pre trip excitement to the camera. I finished of my preparations then headed for bed.

I slept well and woke with that great feeling you have when you are about to embark on a trip. It's hard to describe but it's a waking with warm feeling in your belly and a smile on your face. I had a couple of work conference calls and some bits and pieces to finish off, and in between I packed the bike.

The bike was looking great sitting fully loaded in my garage. The poor weather forecast from the night before was correct so far as I dodged the rain between house and garage. Finally it was 11am, my out of office mail and voicemail was set, and I was ready to go. Amber took a couple of photos, and we hugged and said our goodbyes, I pulled the clutch in and headed out into the rain, the ride to the Midnight Sun had begun.

Day 1 (Friday) 159 Miles

I had my waterproof over suit and recently purchased waterproof mitts on to help combat the rain. The suit was fine but within the first few hundred yards I discovered that I didn't like the lack of feeling on the throttle that came with the mitts; I decided I prefer wet gloves than the lack of feeling. I didn't want to pull over straight away though, I would do it later.

The rain was heavy as I joined the M74 heading south and the wind was quite severe. I was a little concerned what it might be like as I crossed over the high section before Abington which is traditionally a catch all bad weather spot; in the end it was fine. Soon after that I stopped and removed my over mitts and switched on my intercom radio. The radio was not much use with reception fading in and out so I switched it back off.

I made good progress and as I got closer to the English border the roads dried up and the sky was cloudy but didn't look like raining. I had a plan to keep going until I was off the M6, then I would stop at one of the many snack vans you find in Lay-bys in England. As I crossed from West to East I was to discover that there were no such snack vans on this road.

I finally pulled into a garage and had a very salty egg sandwich on poor quality bread, still it filled me up. I watched people going about their normal lives, filling up their cars and heading off. It was a normal day for them I presumed but not for me I thought, I am going on an adventure. I was willing someone to ask me where I was going so I could share it but it never happened. A few miles up the road a snack van smiled at me as I passed it.

I entered the outskirts of Newcastle and while the Garmin was leading me on the same route as the ferry signs I did not recognise the name. I thought it was South Shields I was supposed to be heading for (it turns out it was North Shields). Slowly a feeling of panic started to creep in. Did I type in the wrong port? I'm heading north, what if it's on the other side of the City. "Calm down" I told myself firmly. You can fuel up and go the five miles to the destination. If it's wrong you have time to go elsewhere.

I obeyed my inner self, stopped for fuel and soon after I was in a large queue of bikes waiting to check-in. Is this going to

Amsterdam I asked the guy in front? "Aye" he said in a rough Scottish voice. The guy with the rough voice was like a ned or a chav as they say in England with a bike so I felt no inclination to expand on the conversation.

The number of bikes was so high due to the Moto GP being held in Assen, in the Netherlands, that weekend. I got talking to a pair of mature gents behind me from Dunfermline. They were headed to Munich, where they would meet their wife's, who were flying down. From there it was on to Croatia on their Kawasaki 1400 touring bikes. They were interested to hear I was off to the Nordkapp, surprised again that I was doing it alone.

Eventually we got the call to move forward, and after passing the ticket and passport control area we were finally herded onboard. I have never been on a ferry with so many bikes packed into one deck. It was very tight with a low roof which made it feel quite claustrophobic. We all started to strap down our bikes and unpack with everybody squeezing past each other doing their stuff.

Eventually I made it out of what felt like an oven, and was directed to my cabin. It was ideal and very similar to the little prison cell experience I had before in a crossing from Rosyth to Zeebrugge for my trip to Switzerland.

After unpacking my overnight bag in the cabin I made my way outside and spotted signs to the Sky Bar. It was at the top of the ship and they used the helicopter landing area as space for an outdoor gathering. I bought myself a five euro Grolsh, found myself a good view point, and stood with my face to the sun that had magically appeared.

The Author enjoying a pre-departure beer

It was a great way to experience the departure on a sunny early evening. I felt content, relaxed and excited about the journey ahead as I observed all around me. There were groups of young guys and girls on stag and hen trips, foreign tourists returning home, couples with kids heading on holiday all having what looked like a good time.

Before finding the Sky Bar I had booked myself into the steak restaurant at 6:30pm. I looked at the other options, including the dreaded buffet, and decided not to slum it. With a couple of Grolsh's on board, I made my way down and had a tasty t-bone steak. The restaurant was quiet and relaxing. After a nosey in the duty free shop, I headed into one of the bars where an American guy was singing country and western. He was very good but I did wonder how he ended up there. How does an American end up performing country and western on a boat between Newcastle and Amsterdam?

I sat for a while, read and had a couple of drinks then retired to my cabin. I opened a card Amber had sneaked into my bag. It said "make yourself proud" and she had written "you already make me proud". I will I thought as I contentedly settled down for the night.

My initial sleep was good but I was soon disturbed by a young bunch of hooray Henry's next door chatting at the top of their voices. I also received a text at 2am from my daughter Stephanie who was travelling in Australia asking when I was going on my trip. As you can imagine it was not the best night's sleep.

Day 2 (Saturday) 422 Miles

In the morning I sorted myself out loudly so as to disturb the hooray Henry's but it didn't seem to make much of an impact. I then made the mistake of going to the breakfast buffet which turned out to be an unpleasant experience with poor quality food and vile tasting coffee. I grabbed a better coffee from the coffee shop where I should have eaten, and stood outside gazing at the ocean.

I started talking to a young German man whom I had seen in the queue with a Triumph Bonneville. He had the pony tail and heavy metal t-shirt of a rocker, but he was a gentle rocker. He had been on a solo trip to Ireland, and despite constant rain had a great time. He explained that he had flooded his bike in the severe weather that had hit parts of the north of England the day before, and he was very lucky to have made the ferry.

Soon it was time to head down to the bike cave and get ready to disembark. I timed it well, by the time I arrived most people were already preparing and had made their way past my bike which stood near the door. First things first, it's still upright, which is great. I then go about my fairly well rehearsed process of preparing to disembark. Bags loaded, Air-Hawke seat pad fitted, neck scarf on, gloves tucked behind the screen, Sat Nav mounted and route selected, helmet sitting on the mirror, jacket across the seat and key in the ignition. All ready waiting for signs of the gangway lowering. When that happens it's on with the jacket, helmet and gloves, mount the bike, ready for the off.

I have my moments, and don't always get it right, but I am streets ahead of my friend Raymond. His idea of bike preparation is gloves on, gloves off as he cannot fasten his helmet. Helmet on and fastened. Helmet off as he has forgotten his earplugs. Earplugs in and helmet on and mount the bike. Dismount the bike and remove gloves to take off the disk lock. Gloves back on and ready to go. That's on a good day.

I chat to the two blokes from Dunfermline while we await the gangway coming down. We are already forty five minutes behind schedule, and I despair at their story of the last time they disembarked. Apparently it was a previous Assen Moto GP weekend, and the police breathalysed every bike rider. I had no fears of the outcome of a breath test but didn't fancy the long delay they experienced. Fortunately as the gangway dropped and they waved us forward, there were no police, just warm sunshine to great us.

What did we do before Sat Nav? I wondered, not for the first time, as I weaved through Dutch streets, following the instructions. I feel comfortable in Holland having worked there for nearly five years and enjoyed looking at the typical Dutch houses and many people cycling in the sunshine.

I eventually came to a bridge that was closed due to road works. Now this was one part of Holland I clearly remembered, and it was a pain in the arse. They seem to close roads for fun. It's never ending, not only do they close them, their diversion signs are worse than useless. Myself and a few others, who were clearly also not local, were left with no clue whether to go left or right. I first of all tried left, but it veered off in the wrong direction so I turned around and took the right, only to join a queue of traffic at a standstill. I asked a guy going the other way and he confirmed I was sitting in a queue in the right direction. A kind lady parked in front of me got out to give me directions. Then a guy on a bicycle shouted something in Dutch, and motioned me to turn around. I smiled and waved him on. Better to be in a queue in the right direction than moving in the wrong direction, I thought to myself. Within a few minutes traffic started moving and I was able to rejoin my route.

When I left the ship the sat nav had registered 423 miles to my designation. I had decided to do it in 100 mile sections with a short break and fuel in between. I actually did 124 miles in the first leg, just to get some momentum.

I pulled into one of the many clean cut Dutch petrol stations, filled her up and indulged in a Kass (cheese) roll and a kroket. I was hoping they would have krokets. They're made of some unthinkable mashed crap but taste excellent, just like scotch pies. You can even get a Mckroket at McDonalds in Holland, which I think is great. I have no idea why they haven't opted for a McPie in their Scottish outlets.

Clogs for sale at a Dutch Filling Station

I pressed on wondering when I would hit Germany. I crossed the Afsluitdijk which is 20 miles long dyke crossing the North Sea. It had a beach and there were lots of people spending a relaxing Saturday cycling, walking and flying kites.

At the far end I had to wait in a queue as they let a long trail of yachts through from one section to the other. It was quite strange, but fun, to watch the procession of masts crossing the road in front of me. I got off and stretched my legs and took my helmet and jacket off to cool down in the hot sun. Before long I was off again.

I noticed that there was a massive amount of modern wind turbines dotted in the countryside for miles of my route and thought to myself, Donald Trump won't be building a golf course here then. He has recently been throwing his toys out of the pram because a proposed off-shore wind farm was to be built close to his luxury golf course. A bit ironic methinks as good old Donald swept away everything in his way to make his project happen.

Soon the road signs became German and I realised I must have sneaked across the border without knowing. I smiled to myself when I saw the AUSFAHRT signs. A number of years back travelling to a Germany v Scotland football match with some workmates from our base in Holland, I had commented after seeing a series of signs, that Ausfahrt must be some size of a place. "That means exit in German, you dodo", said Shane the

Australian I was travelling with. They brought it up on a regular basis after that.

The route through Germany was much like Holland, flat, neat, industrial with wind turbines. The added attraction was the Autobahns with no speed restriction. I had listened to my new found Dunfermline friend that 90-100mph was a good speed, in the right conditions and also to my German friend (the gentle rocker) that a circle with a diagonal strip meant 'give it wellie'! So as soon as I saw the sign I duly obliged and cranked it up to 95mph with a few ton toppers, just because I could. The road was dual carriageway, so nothing special but the pace soon became the norm and being slowed down by traffic to eighty was irritating. Still flash and not so flash cars passed me like I was standing still.

The big Beemer took it in its stride but the main lesson I learned was overtaking. Normal process is mirror, lifesaver manoeuvre. Lifesaver is glancing behind you to check the mirrors blind spot. The problem is you have to do it much earlier due to the speed involved. Initially I did the lifesaver then looked back and was on top of the car in front. It did not take long to sort that out.

I passed Dresden, and then finally passed through the very industrial looking Hamburg, heading north towards Denmark. I stopped off at a rest area to look at my texts. One was from my friend Jim (The Moose) wondering when I would be heading off on my trip, another was from my brother telling me about his trip out with my parents that day. He said that my dad, who is eighty one and struggling with his health, had not done well, and said himself that he was unlikely to attempt it again. I wasn't surprised but felt sad for both him and my mother, who despite having a heart attack is still fairly active. I reflected on my dad taking me for rides on my old BSA Bantam while I impatiently awaited my 17th birthday. Life moves at pace I thought, all the more reason for doing things like this.

I pulled out and moved on. I was excitedly awaiting the sat nav showing 156 miles to go. That's a magic number as it represents the mileage from the village I grew up in New Cumnock to our regular holiday destination of Blackpool. For some reason I take comfort in travel by relating distances to New Cumnock routes.

Driving down the 101 in California, I would roar New Cumnock to Ayr with 21 miles to my destination. Still do, always will.

The 156 and 21 mile markers passed by with cheers, I pulled off the motorway and made my way along quiet country roads to the Hotel Kløver in Hellevad. It felt good to be off the highway and so close to my destination. The hotel was set in a neat little village just of the main street and the rain was just coming on as I pulled in to the deep gravel car park.

It's always a good idea to take it easy on a gravel car park especially if people are sitting dining outside watching you. The opportunity for a humiliating fall is high; thankfully I was ok. I did drop one of my good quality gravel coloured earplugs in the gravel. I quickly gave in looking for it. I checked in and advised the receptionist with her distinct dyed bright red hair that I would be leaving early. She told me they did not start until 8am, would I have my meal and settle the bill that night? That was fine by me.

My room was basic, but light and clean and well worth the £58 I had paid for it. I felt as if I wanted to rush back out, and had to tell myself to slow down, relax and enjoy the moments. I did just that and had a shower before wandering along to the restaurant where I enjoyed a nice fish dish in a covered area outside.

It was relaxing sitting there eating as a heavy shower soaked my bike. I organised my panniers, did a little writing, and headed off for an early night. It was not until the early hours of the following morning I discovered that the room didn't have curtains; I was awaked by the dawn. I would have more of that to contend with further north.

Day 3 (Sunday) 209 Miles

I woke up at 6:30am and was on the road at seven complete with rain suit, as it was dry but threatening. I stopped off for my first Danish petrol and joined the highway just as the heavens opened and it continued on and off as I headed north. Quite quickly I could feel water running inside my boots. That soggy wet feeling would be with me on a few more occasions during the trip. Progress was good and I ate up the miles thinking of Amber tucked up cozy in bed on a Sunday morning.

After 100 or so miles I pulled in for breakfast. The girl who served me was a tad grumpy reminding me of Rosie my step daughter when I am running her to work on a Saturday morning. Early morning working and teenage girls don't seem to mix. Maybe my request for a hot dog at 8:30am irritated her, as she pointed to the bread, cheese and ham and grunted. So black coffee, bread and cheese it was and I enjoyed it.

I continued my journey with one short fuel stop and was soon entering Hirtshals on the north coast. It was a much smaller place than I had imagined and I found the ferry terminal with ease and joined the queue. It was a bit DIY to find the biker area, but find it I did. It was a hell of less busy than the Newcastle ferry with only around 10 bikes.

I took my waterproof suit off and emptied a cup full of water out of each boot much to the amusement of the foot passengers waiting to board. I reflected on the fact that this was where I was supposed to meet Willie. I imagined him there with a grin on his face astride his old Honda Dominator. It would have been a strange place to meet him.

They called us forward, and I got the bike strapped down and made my way upstairs to reception. They informed me the cabins were not ready so I found a spot and changed my socks and shoes and read until they finally gave us the nod. When they did I walked through the maze of cabins and eventually found mine.

It was more spacious than the previous, and I had paid for a window. This will do just fine, I thought to myself. The rest of the day was a mixture of dozing, walking on the deck and wandering around the duty free shop. Having been told about the high price of alcohol in Norway by many people, I decided to buy some little bottles of wine and a half bottle of Drambuie. This sweet warm liquor was not something I would normally buy, but they sold it in half plastic bottles which fitted my needs.

Drying my boots

Soon it was 6pm and I made my way up for dinner. It turned out to be my nemesis, a buffet and not the steak dinner I had in my head. However it was Scandinavian, and great quality with delicious fish, beef, cheese, sweets and wine on tap. I filled myself up, and then checked with the host to see if they were showing the Euro football final. "Sure" he said "in the nightclub, but go early as there are 700 passengers and only 300 seats".

Off I went and took a good seat, one hour early, as it filled up around me. Was my time alone affecting me already? I thought to myself, feeling overwhelmed by the throngs of people. The first half was good with Spain 2-0 in the lead, despite all the hard work coming from the Italians. At half time I mulled over getting another beer and staying put, but in the end opted for the quiet of my cabin. I tried to get the second half on the radio, but the pre-paid Internet service was crap. I ended up reading and watching part of a downloaded movie before falling asleep.

Day 4 (Monday) 351 Miles

Just after midnight there was an announcement; we were approaching Stavanger. I sleepily recalled that the ferry stops there on the way. I grabbed my ear plugs and stuffed them in, which did the trick nicely as the next thing I knew it was 4am and I was fully awake. I looked out of the window and could see some little islands and a grey looking morning. I assumed we must be in a fiord, as my cabin faced west.

I started to get ready to take a walk on the deck just before 6:30am when an announcement declared that we would be in Bergen at 8am, and that breakfast was being served. I made a beeline for my pre-paid buffet, and was one of the first in. I love being first when all the food is set out neat and untouched. I had a great time starting with some fruit, followed by soft boiled eggs, salmon and the most delicious well done bacon you could imagine. I had fresh bread and a selection of cheeses washed down with fresh orange juice and hot black coffee.

I had a look at what some of the Norwegians were eating; some of the fish choices had tentacles and eyes. I imagined my eldest son's Justin's reaction to it. I am very sure it would have been "yuck" as the same man considers eating an orange too adventurous.

The earlier announcement had also directed us to vacate our cabins by 7:30am, so after breakfast I contently went back and packed up. I took me and my gear up to the top of the ship and found a great little spot to watch the approach to Bergen. It was beautiful with lots of islands and multi coloured houses built on the cliffs overlooking the sea. The sun came and went a few times as I stood there but it looked decidedly rainy.

A Dutchman in cycling gear also found my spot and asked me to take a picture of him with his camera. I did, and he returned the favour. He was from Utrecht and said he had a stressful job so he was taking three weeks which he called "my time". He told me he had a girlfriend back home, and they had three young children so he was grateful for her support. We exchanged views on the subject of "my time" and agreed it should only add to a relationship, not take away.

Entering Bergen

We both made our way down to the car decks and at first I struggled o find my bike after getting disorientated and going to the exact opposite corner of the deck. Finally I squeezed my way past the cars to my bike.

I went through the off boarding process then chatted to some fellow travelers. First up was a retired couple from Zurich on a Harley. They were also going to the Nordkapp. "How long do you have?" he asked. I said two weeks from now, to go and get back, to Scotland. He repeated my words, followed with "you better hurry and get going then!". He told me that he and his wife were taking four weeks.

Then it was an English guy around my age on a fully laden Yamaha scooter. His name was Steve Taylor, an ex world superbike mechanic who has multiple sclerosis; now he travels all over the world, sponsored by Yamaha, in aid of a Multiple sclerosis charity. He told me he writes an article for the Scooter magazine, Twist and Go. I admired his courage, and his cause, and will certainly look out for his Norway article.

Soon the doors were lowered and we all disembarked via a very steep and slippery looking metal ramp. The rain held off as we queued at customs, until finally they waved us through. Straight away I was confronted by a marching band of youths dressed in blue military style uniforms. I waited by the kerb side while they marched by, trumpets blowing and drums a-beating.

After a short while I was on my way, except I wasn't, as it started raining heavily and I had to pull over to get my rain gear on. Again I cheered loudly to myself that I was on my way, except I wasn't. At least not in the right direction; I had taken the wrong tunnel and was heading south. It was one of those bloody frustrating moments as you try to get back on track in a new city, in the pouring rain; finally I did with a huge sigh of relief.

I should not have worried about my rain suit, as most of the first part of the journey was spent in tunnels, but boy it was a gorgeous country. There were wooded hills and Fjords with Mountains in the distance; it was truly picture postcard stuff.

The speed limits were interesting at eighty kph or fifty mph, but in a way very freeing. Almost everyone obeys them to the letter of the law. You would see the odd maverick doing 55mph, but nothing more. No pressure to crack on, plenty of time to practise smooth lines in the bends and also take in the amazing scenery. I could not believe how everyone stayed in line and I ended up being passed once and passing two people the whole day.

My first goal was Dale, where I needed to decide whether or not to take a mountain detour. When I got there I decided not to for two reasons. One was the weather; the other was the description that it was where the rich Bergen's had their holiday homes. It was wild country I came to see not poseurs playgrounds. Next up was Voss; that had been described as a good stop off point. It looked nice with neat streets filled with interesting shops, but I grabbed some fuel and kept moving on.

My next stop was at the amazing Tvinde waterfall, by the roadside just outside of Voss. What was even more amazing was there was a campsite right below it (on dry land of course). The noise was deafening, and I could not imagine how anyone could possibly sleep through it. I bought some coffee at a kiosk stuffed with cheap tourist gifts, took some pictures and texted Amber to say I was in Norway.

After that I joined route 13 which would take me over my first mountain pass of the day. The weather had brightened up and I was faced with some more spectacular countryside with a mixture of ocean, snow capped mountains and rushing rivers. I stopped off at a view point and wandered around taking shots until a couple pulled up in a Volkswagen and spoiled my peace.

A Golf getting in the way

I then continued up to the summit where the snow was deep on both sides of the road. I switched on the heated grips and thought back to the time before they existed. I remember as a boy in my winter commute to work (21 miles New Cumnock to Ayr!) when I would stop halfway and stuff my gloves on the engine casings so I could feel my hands again. I was a real biker then!

I descended from the mountain; the air warmed up the lower I got. Finally I was back at sea level in village named Vik. It was located in an incredible setting nestled at the mouth of the Sognes Fjord which is the largest Fjord in Norway. I bought a take away coffee and a delicious hot dog from a small store and watched the world go by. I do like a hot dog. I appreciate that's not necessarily a good thing rather like krokets, but still I like a hot dog and Norway likes them too. There was a young couple sitting on a bench eating ice cream. I asked them to take a picture of me and the girl duly obliged.

I moved on along the edge of the Fjord until I came to Vagsnes at the end of the road and a ferry stop. Two young girls stood there in this wonderful setting taking the ticket money. I watched them chat and glance at their mobiles as they do the world over. I guess it's like all things if you live there you are used to it, but I can think of a lot worse jobs (in the summer).

The ferry was ready to go in no time at all and the crossing took fifteen minutes. I was surprised that they didn't tie the bike down and I had a scary moment at the other side as we pulled in to disembark. I was sitting on the bike and suddenly there was this jerk that had me straining to keep it upright. I tensed as I awaited another jerk and sure enough it came. That surely has to knock some bikes over.

We arrived at Hella and I was now riding route 55. The ride was fantastic along the side of the Fjord with great views around every corner. At one point they had put a few cones on the road where the oncoming lane had fallen into the sea. I was gob smacked, that this is how they had dealt with it. Remind me never to ride on a dark wet night in Norway.

A cruise ship was docked at Skjolden at the head of the Fjord. I thought to myself that this location was probably where my brother and his wife docked on their Norway cruise. I passed passengers who must have been let out for good behavior, and felt quite the adventurer with my three day stubble and my two day t-shirt. A few of them glanced at me as I rode by. I wondered if any might have secretly envied the lonesome biker heading north towards the Arctic.

Next up was the Jotunheimen Mountains, or the home of the Giants in English, which is Norway's highest main road mountain crossing. As I approached it the weather looked as though it was closing in. Will I go for it, or should I make camp here for the night and cross tomorrow, I wondered to myself.

That took me back to a time a few years ago when I was on my annual "Oot loose wae a Moose" tour or translated "Out loose with a Mouse" tour. 'The Moose' Jim and I met while we worked in a manufacturing plant in Scotland. Jim also had a passion for bikes and still does but sadly his riding was cut short by a horrific accident where he lost his leg. We drifted apart as we both went through marriage break ups and my change in career so it was 15 years or so before we got together again. It felt as if it was 15 minutes rather than 15 years as we caught up with our lives. We agreed that as a minimum we would take off to the north of Scotland by bike for an overnight catch up each year. It was on our second trip we decided to go to Applecross which involves the only Alpine crossing in the UK. As we approached the weather looked very dark, and the Moose was concerned. I calmed him down and off we went. As we neared the summit the wind was howling like something out of Scott of the Antarctic. It was that whistling sound you get in a gale on TV and the bike was being seriously buffeted about with a steep drop to our left. The other problem was we were in the clouds so I could barely see a few feet in front of me. I can tell you I was one relieved man as we came down the other side into calmer weather. As for the Moose, he was in shock and vowed never again. The next morning the weather looked better so I asked "Which way Moose?" He didn't have to reply; the look told me the coast road, or you will be wearing your bike.

Back at the Giant Mountains crossing in Norway, I didn't have to think for too long; of course I would go for it. The ride up consisted of lots of hairpin bends with diminishing vegetation the higher I climbed. First there were trees, then shrubs, then rocky grass and then bog. I reached the snow line as I neared the summit. In the end it turned out to be much better than the Applecross climb despite being more than two times higher at 1434 metres. It was however bloody cold, wet and misty at the summit so a big enough challenge.

Up in the clouds

Again it was great to get back to lower ground and feel the sunshine hit my face. My destination before leaving on the trip was Otta, just where route 55 hits the E6 but when I arrived I felt as if it looked a bit shabby so I decided to press on to a village named Dombas. The final twenty or so miles were hard as I was feeling very weary. I think one of the disadvantages of travelling alone is there is no one to say "stop we have gone far enough". Maybe it is something you learn with experience.

I eventually came into the village where I located a campsite called Midtskog and for a fee of 150 NK - around £15 secured a pitch. I was tired and hungry as I pitched the tent, and cursed the fact that I had put the poles in the wrong way round. The good news was the sun was beating down, and there were beautiful snow topped mountains in the distance. Finally the tent was up, and the gear was organised.

As it was 8pm, rather than try and cook, I decided to walk to the tourist area for a bite and a beer. Everything was new or under construction, looking like a mini American town with a row of shops/gas stations on each side of the highway. I walked into the Pizza place, and found it to be of a kind of fast food style. I ordered the Burger menu with a beer which sent the waitresses into overdrive. How can you enter number 4 with a beer instead of a coke? I imagined they were saying. I was given a ticket 124 and told my number would be called. The young girl must have read my mind as I wondered what 124 is in Norwegian. She brought my £6 beer straight away and after a while she delivered number 124 by hand, to the annoyance of the other patrons. It has its advantages sometimes being old and uni-lingual. The burger was interesting as it's the first burger I've had smothered in prawn Marie sauce, but hey I was hungry, and wasn't for complaining. I did think to myself that I would have to review my eating habits as the trip progressed.

After that I picked up a lighter, some bread and cheese for breakfast from a supermarket next door then walked back to my tent. I slapped on some skin so soft; if it can repel the Scottish midge the Norwegian mosquito had no chance I reckoned. I sat on my camping chair, smoked a cigar and sipped some wine, reading about the next day ahead in the Arctic Highway book. I then came upon back to hints and tips section. Always carry a spare key it said. That was a good point I thought, and it continued to worry me throughout the rest of the trip.

Day 5 (Tuesday) 310 miles

The wine worked well and I had a good sleep, although I was a little cold during the night. I awoke just before 7am with the sun warming the tent. I boiled some water on the new compact stove Amber had bought by request for Xmas. It was a tiger of a stove compared to the old stuff I used. It roared and brought the water to the boil in no time at all. I overdid the water to coffee ratio, so it was quite weak but it was a lesson learned. I sipped my weak coffee, scoffing my bread and cheese. I methodically packed up everything to the sound of a woman who has clearly smoked too much coughing away in the background. It was a wonderful sunny morning and I felt good.

The ride out of Dombas involved a steep climb up onto Dovrefjell plateau which is national park. It was absolutely perfect in the morning sunshine. I raised my visor to breathe in the fabulous fresh air. I sang at the top of my voice. My son Liam takes spontaneous singing from me, but unfortunately he picks moments like getting ready for work at 6am, rather that alone on a motorbike to do his stuff.

I stopped off at a lay-by just to take it all in, it was so uplifting. I stood there tasting the fresh air in my breath, loving the view and appreciating the silence. This time I was disappointed to descend to the valley but it had to be done. I stopped off at a grass roofed cafe and rested my weary bum. After my coffee I tried to be healthy and buy a single tangerine but after a full five minutes they still couldn't work out a price. In the end I said "just leave it" but it was bizarre.

From there on the route to Trondheim and beyond effectively took me through what I would describe as my trips central belt. Unfortunately all trips seem to have a central belt. It's the bit that's boring and uninteresting sometimes even ugly but you have to do it to get there, or get back. Scotland has a bleak central belt between Glasgow and Edinburgh; my trip to Switzerland had a central belt including parts of northern Switzerland and France. They all have them but I must admit Norway's central belt was the prettiest yet. It's all relative.

Not far beyond Trondheim was a village named Hell. My experience of Hell when I pulled off at the junction was a shopping mall and a Hotel which was as close to real Hell as I could get. I guess I must have missed the village. I did try and find a postcard to send back but there were none to be found. At least I can now say with sincerity that I have been to Hell and back.

The ride got much more interesting as I left the Trondheim commuter belt, and at last I felt a sense of wilderness again. It was mile after mile of forests, rivers, lakes, fjords and twisties. I stopped off at a tourist area with a wildlife park, but moved on without dismounting.

I was conscious of my urge to eat miles, but I had to make sure I took some rest and savor the trip. With my Sat Nav showing 99 miles to Mo i Rana, I spotted what looked like a good campsite on the left, called Sveinningdal Camping. I had missed the turn off so I did a u-turn a little further up the road and made my way back.

The campsite looked well organised and clean, as I did my customary circuit to check it out. It had a mixture of cabins, motor homes and caravans with space for camping. At that point there was only one tent and the sky was ominously grey and I had already noticed a spot or two of rain on my visor. I made my way to the reception and was greeted by a pensive looking lady. "Do you have a cabin" I enquired? She looked at me as if weighing me up. Good biker or bad biker. After a little pause she said "Yes its 300NK (around £30) for the night". "Perfect" I replied, filled in the form, paid the money and took custody of the key.

Cabin 3 looked onto the fast flowing Sveinning River with snow capped mountains beyond. The inside of the Cabin was basic but had cooking facilities and a seating area as well as a sleeping area for two. No bed linen was provided and there was no running water. This will do for me, I thought to myself.

Cabin 3

I took the time to sort out my luggage. First of all emptying the pannier bags and rearranging them, followed by the dry bag. I did my routine bike maintenance checking the tightness of the screen bolts, wind deflector, side stand extender and oil level. I did a little movie shot of the hut then wandered around a little, feeling very chilled in general.

I returned to the Cabin and had a few glasses of very tasty red wine from the 2 bottle bag I had bought in Marks and Spencer back home. I must admit with the Norway pricing and the distinct lack of pubs, that was a very wise move. I fell asleep with a little red wine buzz, to the sound of the river in the background, bliss.

Day 6 (Wednesday) 270 Miles

As usual I was up early in the morning, made coffee on the stove then wandered out to have a shower. It was all quiet except for the river which was roaring away in the background. I noticed a Harley with a little trailer parked by reception and on closer inspection discovered it was from Australia. Now that's what I call a long journey, I thought, as I took a couple of pictures.

I packed up my gear then went back over to reception to see if I might leave the hut key as I had noticed earlier that they were closed. There seemed to be no obvious place as there was no key drop box or letter box, or at least I couldn't find any. I decided to leave the key in the hut and leave it unlocked, as I was sure that would be a safe option.

I was ready for the off as I rummaged in my pockets for my bike key. You know the feeling. Trouser pocket one, it's not there, no worries. Trouser pocket two hmm I thought it might be there, slight concern. Jacket pocket one it better be there, shit it's not, let the panic begin. Jacket pocket 2, please let it be there, no its not. Oh my god I am doomed, dreams destroyed 100 miles from the Arctic Circle. My earlier worries over the tip to carry a spare set of keys had come back to haunt me.

I ran back inside the hut frantically searching to no avail. I took some deep breaths and decided to retrace my earlier steps to reception. I checked around the Aussie Harley, then the reception area with no apparent letter box, and finally wandered across the gravel area back towards my hut. Suddenly I saw the keys lying on the gravel. I kissed them in relief and the stress flowed out of my body as I inserted them into the ignition. Thank you rushing river god, thank you, I muttered.

I had already decided that I would have breakfast on the road as I moved off. My fuel was quite low so I checked the Sat Nav for a petrol station within range and a few options popped up about 20 miles or so further north. En route I experienced Norwegian road works which were very interesting. They basically rip the top off the road and tell you to slow down (even more). It was standing on the pegs stuff for the GS which made it enjoyable but I felt sorry for the poor camper vans bouncing along.

Standing on the pegs took me back to a trip I made with the Moose on pillion a few years back. There are several reasons for standing on the pegs the most common being to stretch your weary legs. Another is if you are on rough ground such as Norwegian roadwork's to give you better control. During that trip I had been standing on the pegs and when we pulled over the Moose enquired "Why do you stand up big fellow, is it to stretch your legs?" "No Moose" I replied. "It's to fart".

I re-fuelled at Mosjoen which was a railway hub set against impressive sheer cliffs. I had a white chocolate cookie for breakfast which was not enjoyable, but the only other choice was a mars bar. I pressed on and the country side became a bit more manicured green with snow capped mountains in the distance. I got stuck behind a line of camper vans and trucks which I slowly passed one by one. To be fair most drivers ushered me through with my headlight and twin spot lights bearing down on them.

The scenery improved by the mile when finally I came upon an E6 road closure with no clear sign of an appropriate detour. I pulled into a rest area and asked a guy who turned out to be Polish for directions. He pointed up the hill, which would have been my second choice of the two available. I asked him to take my picture as the view was great. He obliged and soon I was on the hill road connecting to the E6 further north. It was a great diversion as it took me to the Korgenfjellet kro & motel which had and a car park with fantastic views of the snow capped mountains.

I chatted to a German bloke who was with his two mates who were on BMW bikes. He took a picture of me with my camera and told me they were Nordkapp bound also. I asked him about the route down and after a conversation in German with an older surly looking guy, he said 5-6 days. I smiled, "oh shit I better go". He laughed and waived me away.

A view from the detour

I had set the Garmin for some obscure address in Mo I Rana as I did not know, but later was advised, if I pressed the arrow down button I could select a city with no address. Anyway the result was I went through Mo I Rana without realizing it, and was heading for some suburb. Luckily I caught on quite quickly, and did a u turn to get back on track.

I was buzzing with excitement as I left Mo I Rana. I was now on the Arctic Highway or the Blood Road. I reveled in the prospect of crossing the Arctic Circle on my own motorbike having ridden it from home. I soon passed the sign for the Arctic Circle race track which I had read was a high quality circuit. It made me smile thinking "build it and they will come".

Despite all the excitement I was also very hungry so when a cafe appeared I pulled over. It was a magical place for three reasons. The first being the excellent hot dog, secondly the excellent omelette with salad and bread and last but not least it had Wi-Fi. This allowed me to top-up both my food and connectivity requirements.

The girl running the cafe was probably in her thirties with short dark hair and had a very kind way of dealing with me. I wondered what it would be like running a cafe this far north. Would it be open all year? I finally packed up my I-Pad, got geared up and moved on.

As I had read, the trees gave way to a much more barren setting, and before long I could see the Arctic Circle centre looming in the distance. I whooped for joy and grinned from ear to ear thinking, you've done it boy, you have ridden your motorbike to the Arctic Circle. I pulled in to the busy car park and parked up. I first of all had my photo taken by a kind looking old couple by the globe shaped monument then wandered up the hill to take a look at a mass of cairns that had been erected. I added a stone to one on behalf of those I love, and just took in the moment. It was the perfect setting with the snow on the hills, the lunar landscape and the wind howling in my ears. I made my way down to the visitors centre and commercial as it is, I enjoyed wandering around the shop picking up a few gifts including Arctic Circle Mints for the kids, a great pair of Reindeer socks for Amber and bike stickers for myself. Finally I decided it was time to head north again.

I have made it to the Arctic Circle

The landscape remained lunar for a while, and then became a little more forested. My Garmin screen became unreadable so I stopped to see what was happening. I could not work it out so I pulled into the Saltdal tourist centre to check it in the shade. For some reason the brightness was turned down to 20%, so I cranked it back up to 100% and I was back in business.

I pushed on and eventually came to a town named Fauske. It was an attractive little town so I parked up on the sea front and read my Arctic Highway book, which recommended a side trip to the town of Bodo. I calculated it was roughly a 50 mile detour in total, which was not too bad. I had read about an impressive tidal current that sweeps all ahead of it and thought that was located at Bodo, but I had misread it; that was elsewhere.

I headed off to see the famous current in Bodo which wasn't in Bodo. The ride was fine along the Fjord edge, until I entered Bodo itself. The town turned out to be a lot bigger than I had imagined, with a population of nearly 50,000 and I ended up in a long traffic jam heading into the centre with no opportunity to turn. By the time I reached the harbour I was frustrated; I had not come north of the Arctic Circle to sit in urban traffic jams. I pulled over and checked my book to discover that I was in the wrong place for the tidal current. I had had enough of Bodo, so I swung round, heading back towards Fauske.

The road back seemed long, and I was getting sore probably heightened by my frustration. I considered staying at a campsite on the outskirts of Fauske, but decided I should make some more miles. This pushing myself on and on became a theme for the trip and in reflection I should have taken a bit more time to enjoy rather than endure.

The scenery beyond Fauske was amazing, with great views looking down into the Fjords and snow capped mountains all around. I stopped off at a lay by and stood on a picnic bench to take pictures. There was a camper van parked there too, and I'm sure they thought I was a bit strange.

Soon after that I came across a road sign for Camping. I rode past it initially, but after a short while I did a u-turn; the location looked great. I first turned into a gravel road which lead me down to what was a former ferry point, now deserted except for a campervan parked up, and a tanned white haired man sitting outside, taking in the sunshine. I asked him if he knew where the campsite was but he couldn't hear me over my engine. I switched it off and asked again, but he just shrugged his shoulders as if saying "I have no idea". I backtracked up the short distance to the main road and turned left looking for another route. Sure enough there was a site, but the road down to it made me question the quality of the site itself, so I moved on.

I stopped for fuel a little further on; I must admit the pay at pump 24x7 services is a great thing, as the little adjoining store was a long time closed.

I can wear the badge

I continued north and within a few kilometers I noticed a sign for Kovatn camping. This had to be the one, I thought, as I felt the aches and pains of the day's journey, mainly in my rear end. I turned down this road to my right, and there was a little reception hut. The campsite looked clean and tidy and was on the side of the Fjord and I decided that this was the place for tonight.

I parked up and went inside to be greeted by a lady in her sixties, who could not speak English. We managed to establish that I was looking for a camping pitch, so she led me outside and pointed to a cracking spot looking onto the Fjord. I was delighted, it was idyllic and I immediately started pitching my tent. There was a Camper van close by, so I pitched it in the best spot to afford us both some privacy. I remembered my frustration of trying to get the tent poles seated a couple of nights before, so this time I actually read the instructions. Pole A, then B and, you got it, C. It worked a treat and before long I had the tent pitched and my contents decanted inside.

If Carlsberg made Campsites

It was a lovely night so I stripped down to my shorts and cooked one of the pre-packed camping meals I had bought in Scotland. Tonight it was the turn of the Chicken Korma, which again turned out to be rather tasty. This was washed down of course with some duty free red wine. It was first equal in my most idyllic camping spots with the mountains being reflected on the perfectly still Fjord as the sun went down. The other one was a pitch on the island of Islay with uninterrupted view of an empty beach and the sea.

The Motor home couple next to me were sipping white wine at a picnic table on the other side of my tent. I asked them to take my picture, and they duly obliged. That got us talking, and they turned out to be from the south of Sweden. The lady looked alarmed when I described my journey ahead, and said "you poor man, two weeks on your own". I just smiled and said "I'm sure I'll be all right".

I then exchanged a few texts with my friend Wilson, he, understandably, was asking if I had photo-shopped my location when I sent him a picture. It was a marvelous location on a marvelous evening and I treasured every minute of it before heading to bed.

Day 7 (Thursday) 302 miles

I woke up on feeling very pleased having stumbled on such a cracking camping location. The air was dry, and so was the tent, so I was very relaxed as I made my coffee and porridge, both of which were delicious. I used the picnic bench the Swedish couple had used last night as a staging post, as I packed up.

I love when I am the only one up in a campsite, and that was the case this morning. It's hard to describe but it just feels good to get organised alone before the shower blocks and kitchens fill up with campers. I finally started the engine, and waving to the closed curtains of the Swedish couple, I was off.

The roads were empty and the scenery uplifting, as I climbed another mountain pass. I passed a sign for Sand, which I decided I must remember so I could orientate myself on the map. I am afraid Sand was another 'Ausfahrt' moment, as a few miles later there was another sign for Sand - this time I noticed the big yellow sand container.

I stopped off at a view point and marveled at the Lafoten Islands in the distance. Willie had described these islands as a magical place. They certainly looked magical from where I stood with their jagged mountain tops. I took a photo of the Moose warning sign, yes those big things with horns. Then I continued down the mountain, emerging at a village named Ulsvag, and had a coffee enjoying a great view from the balcony.

Do I go to the Lofotens now or not I mulled. Willie had said you must go to the Lofotens, to a place named "A" but I knew it was a long detour. As I checked the map I noticed there were two ferries at Bognes, one to Lodingen and the continuation of the E6 but also one to Svolvaer on the Lofotens. I searched for A on the map but could not find it.

When I arrived in Bognes I had half an hour before both ferries arrived. I checked with the staff after a searching hard to locate one, and discovered it was a one hour crossing to Svolvaer on the Lofotens. Why does every one go on about it being a massive detour, I wondered? Ok now my mind was made up, I must do the Lofotens.

The ferry journey brought some further stunning views, although once again they did not tie my bike down, which made me nervous. I got chatting to a scruffy Norwegian with a lovely mongrel dog. He explained he was delivering him to a new owner. Lucky person I thought to myself I hope they appreciate him.

A view from the ferry

We docked up with the bike still standing upright, and I pulled in to a service station, located at the harbor, for some pizza and coffee. It was tasty and well priced.

I made my way out to discover the Lofotens, and within a few minutes saw a sign for A which was 230 kilometers. I was really struggling now in my mind what to do. I pulled over to think. That's a good 240 miles round trip, I thought, one hell of a detour. Could I do it? What would that do to my Nordkapp arrival date? Is it worth it? In the end I made the worst decision of all, no decision. I kept edging on, unconvinced.

It leaves you in a hellish position of uncertainty, or at least it seemed to for me. I needed to know what the next few hours would bring. Fatigue was fighting curiosity, the scenery was brilliant, but could it possibly get better? As I craved a coffee, I decided to myself that if anyone wanted to start a money for old rope business, then opening a coffee shop within the first 50 miles of getting off the Svolvaer ferry is a great bet. Just a stall with a few added extras, like a hot dog, would have them, (and me) coming in their droves.

I edged on towards A and, fairly early on, went through a 6.4 kilometer tunnel. The amount of money spent on engineering projects in this country is amazing although I suppose if you charged between six and seven pounds for a beer in Scotland we could do the same, actually probably more.

I then came upon an undersea tunnel, now these worry me. Its bad enough passing under the Clyde in Glasgow, but the thought of an ocean above my head scares the hell out of me. I get nervous as I hit the bottom, and for no logical reason accelerate up the hill to avoid the torrent of escaping sea water. The sat nav does not help, as it highlights the fact I am actually in the ocean.

Amazingly I emerged safe, and soon I pulled into a view point filled with common garden camper vans. There were wooden steps going up to an elevated view, so I chose that option." Truly amazing scenery but is it worth going to A?" I pondered. I took some movie footage, but timed it with the arrival of a couple who destroyed my solo moment.

When I came down another GS pulled in. It was yellow, and had a German plate. I waved, and he waved back, parking up a few spots along. He must have sensed that I was desperate to talk to him, so made his way to another view point. Eventually he came past me, with his Enduro helmet still on, and said Hi. He had a gaunt face, and seemed a little uncomfortable about making conversation. I asked him which direction he was going, and he told me he had just come from A. "Is it far?" I asked, "and where exactly is it, because I can't find it in my map?" He pointed to the most southerly edge of the Lofotens and said "there" with a smile.

"It took me 12 hours to get down as I followed the yellow roads" he said, pointing to the map. "Then 4 hours on the main road".

Bloody hell I thought, at least that's one decision made. I will stay clear of the yellow road. He recommended a campsite just down the road and then we parted ways. I past the campsite, and soon entered Svolvaer where the scenery was awesome, and fuel and food were served.

I pulled into a petrol station, and found I couldn't get my helmet to flip up. I kept pulling away at it, to no avail; one side was definitely stuck fast. I managed to get my glasses off, and wrestle the helmet from my head. Still I had no luck in getting it to flip. I wrestled it back on and then found there was no way to get my glasses on. Shit, I had a problem. I would need to remove the flip part. I was sweating with the efforts and felt stressed. It looked like two Allen head bolts, so I took off my bag and chair, and removed the rear and front seat to get to the tool kit; nothing fitted. I asked myself, what would the big bike adventure man do?

First he would check the Shell shop for tools. Nope that didn't work as there did not sell anything beyond a torch. . Then he would go across the road to the service place and ask to borrow an Allen key. Off I went, but the workshop was empty. I was tempted to rummage through the tools but resisted. After a few circuits of the building I asked a man unloading boxes if he worked there. He looked relieved I was only after a tool and not an engine rebuild, and located the right thing very quickly. I looked at the flip part after removing it, and opted for the bin as it was so messed up. Off I went again, still heading unconvincingly to A.

With all the helmet hassle in Svolvaer, I had forgotten to eat. I was very hungry, tired and a bit irritated with myself. I almost knew I would keep going all the way to A, but my body didn't want to. I followed a sign for food but ended up in a slow queue of traffic on a single road, at which I did a u-turn in frustration, and re-joined the main route. After quite a distance I found a café, and had the special, a chicken curry wrap which went down a treat. I felt better, and with it I had also discovered a possible campsite for the night.

As I pressed on, a plan started to form in my head. I will go on to A, return to the chicken curry wrap campsite for the night, then head off early in the morning.

The scenery had changed into almost flat suburban, and I was concerned that it would be like that all the way to A. What was driving me there was not just a tick in the box, but the thought that I might miss something even more spectacular than the scenery I had already ridden through. I passed a big modern Viking museum on my left, its parking lot filled with tour buses and cars. Was it not for my quest I might have stopped off and enjoyed that?

Eventually the scenery returned as I made my last miles towards A. There were impressive rocks, Lord of the Rings style Mountains, coast and islands joined together by short bridges.

Just 5 kilometers outside of A I was held up for a good 10 minutes at road works. Finally we were waved through and I entered A, which was similar to the many villages I had passed. I pulled up beside a Finnish couple on a bike, who ignored my greeting. I wandered around the car park for a minute or two, then thought ok I've done A, let's go.

I followed two Norwegian bikers riding Suzuki's for a short spell, and stopped behind them at the road works. One got off and chatted to me. They were on a four day 'boy's' bike tour. The skies were getting dark by now and a few spits of rain were falling. "Looks like rain suit time" I said to the guy. "No no" he replied "look the sky is blue over there".

We moved on, and after another kilometer I pulled over in the torrential downpour to don my rain gear. I had noticed this place on my way to A, with its adverts for delicious hamburgers. It turned out it was a very up market fish shop, and the hamburger was actually some kind of cold fish burger. I resisted the temptation and moved on.

Suddenly a solid plan came into my head. As its raining, I will head back to Svolvaer and get a hotel room. I will have a nice meal, and perhaps the draft beer I have been yearning for. I felt good but sore as I made the 60 or so miles back past the boring area, the Viking museum and the planned chicken curry campsite. By the time I reached Svolvaer I was knackered, and needed fuel. I bought a hot dog, just in case it took a while to get settled and find a restaurant.

Once I had something to eat the thought of a hotel became less appealing, as it had dried up and the sun was out. I remembered the German biker telling me earlier that the campsite not far from here was good.

I pressed on, and soon arrived at the campsite which was called Hammerstad Sjohuscamping. It must have been around 9pm when I arrived: it looked pretty busy and there were a few bikes around. The friendly owner said they were full, but he would try and find me a corner. Sure enough he did and it was literally a small piece of the gravel road. I gave up trying to put pegs in, but was ok with it as it was a calm night- there should be no issues.

A gravely spot

There was a car next to me, then a tent with a white guy and his Asian wife, partner or whatever. He looked at me suspiciously as I set up camp. As the night went on I got the feeling the lady was unhappy in some way, which could, of course, all be in my imagination. Next to them were a bunch of German bikers, all sitting around a table, drinking beer. They acknowledged me but didn't look like they wanted to engage any further.

I took a shower after what had been a long day and then sat in the kitchen area charging up my i-phone and making use of the Wi-Fi as some young Dutch people cooked a meal. I decided on an alcohol free night, and went off to rest my weary bones.

Day 8 (Friday) 276 Miles

I was awoken by the wind and the rain buffeting the tent during the night, not ideal I noted, with no tent pegs. I moved the heaviest items I had into each corner then drifted back to sleep.

I awoke again around 5am, and tossed and turned, thinking it was too early to get up and disturb everyone. The rain was still battering the tent, but I knew I had the nightmare job of packing up the tent in the wet. I was as organised as I could be, doing as much of the preparation inside the tent as I could, but still it was a miserable task. I knew once I was on the bike I would feel better. So at 6am I fired up the Beemer and got out of there as quick as possible, no doubt with a trail of angry muttering campers left in my wake.

I then had to make a choice between two routes. The one my Sat Nav was pointing me to was for a ferry departing from a little further north in the island, landing near Narvik where I could rejoin the E6. The other was to go back the way I had come, and take a second ferry to Lodingen, and the continuation of the E6. I had read that the first 15 kilometres of the second route were possibly the most scenic part of the Arctic Highway. The problem was that with the cloud and rain, you couldn't see a thing anyway. Clearly the Narvik route was the more sensible choice, but I was here to do the Arctic highway, and do it I would, so I opted to go back and join the road where I left it.

As I made my way back to Svolvaer for the ferry, I saw an animal on the road ahead. I was not sure what it was, but as I slowed down it ran towards me. Just a few feet before it reached me this beautiful Beaver veered to the side, and scurried off into the long grass. I was delighted by that and later discovered from Norwegians that it was a very unusual thing to see.

It continued to rain heavily as I retraced my steps, and finally arrived back at the Pizza serving service station. I ordered a coffee and a bun, and settled down in the cafe area. I had 45 minutes or so to wait for the next ferry. It was good just to chill there out of the rain. I bought myself a hot breakfast and a little oil funnel as I was sure at some point the Beemer would need a top up, though it turned out not to be the case. After half an hour I joined the ferry queue in the rain, and soon we were boarded and away. This time I stayed inside drinking coffee, and eating a delicious petite salmon and tomato sandwich at a cost of £7.50.

The ferries were timed to perfection, and I rolled off one and onto the other. During the short crossing, I smiled to myself thinking about a trip I had taken to the Scottish highlands a month earlier. I was doing a circuit of Skye with my friend Wilson. We were catching a local ferry for a very short crossing between Skye and the mainland at Glenelg. This is a small community owned ferry and is the last manually operated turntable ferry in Scotland. As Wilson and I stood beside our bikes on the ferry awaiting departure, he casually asked "When do you think the next ferry will arrive"? I looked at him blankly then said "We're on the ferry*."I thought this was the Pier" he replied laughing. I have to give him some credit it's a small flat ferry, but it's definitely not a pier.

I rejoined the highway at Lodingen, and sure enough I could not see a thing as I crossed the most scenic mountain pass, I felt disappointed but it was as expected. As I approached Narvik it felt like I was in another central belt area as the landscape became very suburban. As I entered Narvik there were story boards concerning the battles that had taken place there during World War II but it was just too wet to stop. I got through Narvik fairly quickly, and then made my way along the coast to Bjerkvick, where I stopped off for fuel, a rest, a coffee and a hot dog. What happened to the healthy eating? The weather was miserable as I sat there perched on a high stool watching people getting on with their daily lives.

There were a couple of bikers sitting nearby but their body language was not welcoming. So far my illusions of biker brotherhood had not materialized. Maybe I was expecting it, or wanting it, too much. Maybe it was because I was so far from home and alone, that I was not trusted. I don't know, but I felt a bit disappointed.

My route out of Bjerkvick took me on a climb past another war memorial. Apparently some of the fiercest fighting in the Narvik campaign took place around this area with Bjerkvick being almost destroyed by Allied warships.

It was a long ride cutting inland over the plateau, and the seascape was left far behind.. The scenery was good, but felt rather bleak in the rain. I eventually came to a town named Setermoen, which was a pleasant enough place, and stopped off at Patricia's Café which was suggested in my Arctic Highway book.

Patricia's cafe

It was a small establishment, mainly geared for the takeaway market, but had a large communal table where I settled and removed my wet gear. I ordered the fish n chips but Patricia (if that was who she was) advised me she was out of fish. As I thought about what I might choose instead, she triumphantly said she had found a fish, and waved a frozen filet at me. "Hmm" I said," its ok. I'll have the Chili Chicken burger instead".

The food was wholesome and filling and the coffee hot. It was just what I needed to recharge my batteries. Patricia asked me about my trip, and was surprised to hear I was doing it alone. "All by yourself" she proclaimed!

I left Patricia's and got back on the road singing "all by myself", passing through a military town named Bardufoss, with a large barracks running along the main street. I kept moving, and came up behind two fairly slow moving bikers with Latvian plates; I gave them a wave as I passed by.

A little later, as I crossed a plateau, I came across my first Sami tourist encampment with tents housing gift shops. There was a heavily equipped BMW GS Adventure, so I parked beside it. It had stickers from Africa, South America and all sorts on it, so I guessed it belonged to a serious biker. I stumbled into him in the first tent, where they had an open fire and a simmering pot of Reindeer soup. He was a middle aged Frenchman who spoke no English. We shook hands, and grunted until we were rescued by his son, who explained to his father I was not Swiss but Scottish. They were on their way back from the Nordkapp. The Latvian bikers pulled in just as we had both mounted up to go our separate ways. It was waves all round then we were off.

Soon after that I decided to start the search for accommodation using my Garmin. There was no way I was tenting it tonight, even though the weather had dried up. I had some seriously wet gear to dry out, ranging from socks, boots, sleeping bag and tent. I registered a hotel around 14 miles up the road that I had read was fairly ok. The thought of a dry room, a comfortable bed and that elusive cold "draft" beer was enticing.

I eventually came across a hotel that looked kind of modern chic in a Norwegian way i.e. not overly modern and chic. I had read that if there were no tour buses in the car park then a deal could be done. I made my way to reception where I was ignored by one guy doing some filing and another on a mobile phone. I was not impressed by this as a starting point as I was already questioning whether this was the right place. Even if they continued to ignore me, should I be spreading wet gear across what I expected would be a clean cut, modern hotel room. Eventually the older guy on the phone gestured to the guy doing the filing to attend me. He offered me a room for £125 for the night, which I didn't want to pay. I half heartedly to negotiate but it was to no avail.

I was now clear a hut would be best, and a little further on I came upon the Stranbu camping site. To be honest it was more of a small holiday park, focusing on static caravans with some space for touring caravans, motor homes and a few Huts. It looked clean and I was ready for a rest, so I checked with reception for availability. At around £65 for a Hut with running water it was at the expensive end, but after a little internal humming and hawing I decided I would go for it.

Once again I was allocated hut three and it was in a really nice location, kind of tucked into a corner backing onto open fields. There were no real views from the windows or balcony, but the snow-capped mountains lay behind. Internally it was excellent, and it even had a small portable television mounted on the wall. I put on an episode of Dallas, in English with Norwegian subtitles, to keep me company as I started the drying out process. It was one room but spacious, with four bunks lining one wall. It had a dining table, lounge chair and a small but functional kitchenette. I rearranged the dining table to hang wet items in front of the hot radiator, and used the empty bunks as a staging post for before and after.

I then wandered over to the shower room, only to find that I needed coins for a shower. This was the norm but still annoying when paying £65 a night. Instead I washed my clothes in the sink free of charge, and took them back to the drying hut. I wandered up to reception and had a general look around. It was a bit like static caravan parks in Scotland, with people creating their home from homes with decking, barbeques and patio furniture. I checked for beer availability in the small supermarket, but, in true Norwegian fashion, it was a resounding no. I got change for the shower, and wandered back to my hut. It was still early, but I was tired, so after a few red wines I was tucked up in bed and soon fell fast asleep.

Day 9 (Saturday) 374 Miles

I awoke to the sun streaming in the window of hut three; it was a good feeling. The bed had been comfortable, and I had managed to dry all of my stuff off on the roasting hot radiator, no doubt built to deal with Norwegian winters. I made my coffee and porridge on the stove and then started packing the bike. I used my change from last night to have a shower. The huts next to me had all been taken while I slept, and I even had a few touring caravans in the grassy area out front. Clearly it was time to move on.

I was determined to camp again that night, if the weather held out; huts, as good as they were, felt like a bit of a cop out. I had planned to wild camp in Norway while I was beyond the Arctic Circle, and I suddenly realized that tonight would be my last chance. I knew I was around 350 miles from the Nordkapp, so I had an outline plan of camping somewhere near Alto. With the bike packed up I tidied up my hut, keeping the reputation of trusted old bikers intact and returned the keys to reception.

I was back in Fjord country now and enjoyed the ride along the beautiful Fjord edge. It was on this route that I encountered my first Reindeer, or two actually, who were wandering along the road and came right past me as I sat stationery. They were big beautiful animals, not something you would want to hit on a bike. The closest Reindeer gave me an indignant look as he ambled by.

Soon after that I passed a Sami tourist encampment where there were guys dressed up in their traditional clothes, but it was heaving with tourists who had recently disembarked from a bus parked nearby, so I kept on moving..

I rode over another high pass, and at the top stopped off at a cafe with another gathering of Sami souvenir tents; this one was nice and quiet. I pulled up beside a gleaming Honda Africa Twin, same colour as Willies. Maybe he's here after all, I joked to myself. It was not to be, as a dour French biker emerged from the cafe, more or less ignored my nice bike gesture and rode off.

I was not ready for a coffee, but did fancy a look in the gift tents. I had a notion to get myself a reindeer skin to use as padding on the bike seat. Not for this trip but for shorter rides at home. I have seen quite a few folks use sheepskins, but reindeer skin seemed a bit more unique and it appealed to my sense of adventure biker come mountain man. In the second tent I was rummaging through the options when a pretty young girl asked in text book perfect English if she could help. I explained what I was after and she patiently explained the different options from a full skin (too large) to an assorted remnant (too small) to the shoulder and back part (just right). We agreed on 12 Euros (yes she did Euros), and the deal was concluded. It fitted the contours of the seat perfectly and I had a lady tourist take pictures of me proudly displaying it on my bike.

Proudly displaying my Reindeer Skin

Just before Alta I stopped off at the Tirpitz museum which was indicated by a low key sign post and was housed up a lane in a large old wooden hut. It turned out to be an excellent experience starting with a film in English detailing the famous battleships stay, just a couple of kilometers down the road, where it was subject an unsuccessful attack by British mini submarines. It later moved further south and was eventually sunk during an air attack. It contained interviews with people of that time, which made it very real and special. The museum was full of excellent artifacts from both the ship, and the period in general.

As I was leaving I asked the curator exactly where she had been docked, and it turned out to be at a narrow point I had just passed where they are currently building a bridge. I decided to back track the couple of kilometers and take a look. There was no obvious place to stop in what was an inactive construction site, but eventually I pulled over onto some rough ground. This place would be heavily signposted with a tourist centre, coffee shops and parking if it were in the UK. Maybe I missed them but I could see no signs letting passersby know that this was such a historic spot.

I went to lean my bike on its side stand when I suddenly realised I had not kicked the stand out. In a nanosecond I was heaving to stop it from falling, veins bulging out of my head with the enormous strain. The last piece of high quality German engineering had not gone down in this spot, and I was damned sure I was not going to let this one go down either. Somehow I managed to stop it on the very edge of the tipping point, and the day was saved. I very methodically positioned the stand down and then took a look at the points on both sides of the Fjord where I had seen the Tirpitz docked earlier in the historical prints. I closed my eyes for a moment and imagined the scene not so many years ago.

I remounted and swept past the museum again, this time heading for Alta. The town itself looked ok, if a little run down. It didn't really appeal to me as a stopping over place and besides, it was still mid afternoon. I did however need to eat, so I pulled into a cafe that had a picnic bench outside in the sun. It was again one of those fast food looking places that Norway seems to specialize in.

There were a couple of other bikes parked up, but their owners didn't look much like they wanted to engage. I decided I would have the Alta special beef burger, to sample the local cuisine. They brought it outside to me served with a little salad and fries. It was the most bizarre beef burger I have ever experienced. It was a beef burger topped with beef! Yes I can say it again, a beef burger with little strips of beef on top, interesting but tasty in an unusual kind of way.

I headed out to Alta, knowing that I would be crossing a windswept plain which was deep in Sami land, and I was relishing it. It was really characterful with a very rugged Arctic feel to it. The landscape reminded me of New Mexico in the winter, with the poor looking Sami huts not unlike the Native American dwellings. It seems to be the same old hard time story all over the world when it comes to indigenous people.

The Sami people inhabit the far Northern parts of Norway, Sweden and Finland and the Kola Peninsula of Russia. They are most famous for their semi nomadic lifestyle of Reindeer herding. In many areas this practice is now a legally protected right for Sami people only. I pulled over to watch a large herd of reindeer wander close to the road and imagined what it might be like in the depths of winter this far north.

I moved on once again with a fierce debate raging in my head. I knew I was approaching a junction at Skaidi where I had a choice of continuing towards the Nordkapp, or turning left and riding 40 or so miles to Hammerfest, Europe's most northerly town. I knew in my heart I could not come this close without visiting Europe's most northerly town, decision one made. I turned left. The route passed through a further number of poor looking settlements as I skirted a large fjord. My mind was again going ten to the dozen wondering if I should stay in Hammerfest, which from a fatigue point of view was most appealing. The only niggling doubt was that it would be great to be at the Nordkapp at midnight, and if I stayed in Hammerfest tonight that would mean a very low mileage day tomorrow. I decided to let Hammerfest make the decision. If it attracted me enough I would stay. I crossed a large suspension bridge and came upon some nice twisties as I neared Hammerfest. I had another great Reindeer moment when another fine specimen took command of the road ahead. Again it just wandered past my stationery bike, giving me a indignant stare on the way past.

Finally I arrived on the outskirts of Hammerfest, where a large model of a Polar Bear welcomed me to the town. I noticed the campsite was closed, so if I did want to stay I was looking at a hotel. I hit some road works and was put on a short diversion, which brought me out on what seemed like the main street. There was nothing wrong with the town, but it certainly wasn't saying stay. I rode up the main street then turned around, stopping off for some pictures of the polar bear before setting off back in the direction I had come from.

Welcome to Hammerfest

My Garmin advised me that I should arrive at the Nordkapp Campsite at around 9:30pm which would position me nicely to make camp, then head up to the Nordkapp centre before midnight. The ride back to the junction at Skaidi passed quite quickly, and I stopped for fuel with under a hundred miles to go.

After a few miles I turned left onto the E69 taking me on my final route north. The scenery was lovely, and the winding coastal road good, but I was very weary after such a marathon day. The route included some undersea tunnels and also the most dimly-lit tunnel of the journey. The final part of the route took me up over high open ground and I was buffeted by strong winds. I caught a glimpse of what I assumed was the north coast and the sun was shining on the water. Maybe I would get to see the Midnight Sun?

After descending from the pass I came across a little row of Campsites nestled around a junction. I looked at the first two and decided the one nearest the road was my preference so I pulled in.

There was a large reception hut which housed an informal restaurant. A lady in her thirties checked me in and pointed me towards a bumpy field, where there was only one other tent complete with a couple of motorbikes. I picked a spot looking down the valley and pitched up. I wasted no time and soon I was on my way on the short drive to the Nordkapp centre. I had been told about the expensive entry fee of over £20, and had also had some negative comments around how commercial it was.

I parked up in the giant car park which was busy with cars and tour buses and headed to the building a few hundred yards away.

Sadly the sun had gone and the sky was looking very grey, but it was still full on daylight as I wandered towards the complex. It was a huge building with several floors containing an I-Max cinema, various restaurants, bars, shops and displays.

My first priority was to head through the centre and out to the iconic metal Globe sculpture, which signaled that I had made my goal. I was buzzing with excitement as I made my approach. It felt great to stand by the globe and I was grinning from ear to ear and congratulating myself silently amongst the crowds. I asked an Italian couple to take my picture, then made my way to the cliff edge and looked out to sea. After ten minutes or so I headed back into the centre and despite some of the negative feedback I must admit I loved the place.

My goal achieved – The Nordkapp

It had such an upbeat atmosphere, and was well laid out. I watched the very well made movie taking you on a journey through the seasons at the Nordkapp. Getting there was hard though, as I picked the same time as an army of Oriental tourists let by an aggressive crazy guy with a flag. He actually physically tried to push me to the side which I could not help but resist. He was a very ignorant man.

After that I went up to the restaurant for a snack and tried to phone home. Irritatingly I had run out of credit, and despite several frustrating attempts I could not top it up. I had hoped to share my moment with Amber, but it was not to be. After that I visited the large gift shop, and bought post cards and a few presents.

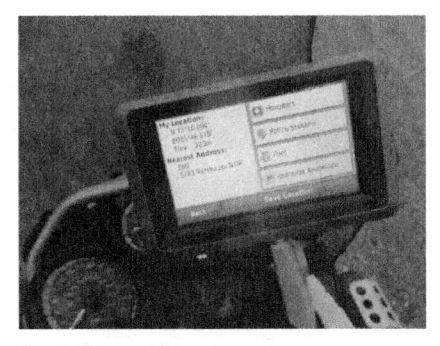

Proof of the pudding

It was approaching midnight now, so I made my way back to the Globe to celebrate the midnight light, as unfortunately all hope of a midnight sun was gone. There were a few people around in the drizzle, but there were no whoops or hollers as midnight struck like you might experience in the USA.

I celebrated internally and made my way back to the centre, and soon after out to the car park in heavy rain. I took some pictures of my milometer which was registering 13,906 miles, and the location N 71 degrees on my Garmin. I had travelled 2,673 miles to reach this spot. Then for the first time in the trip I started heading home. The light was amazing despite having no sun, as I made the short journey back to my tent. Once in and settled, I did a proper toast with a large Drambuie then contentedly fell asleep.

Day 10 (Sunday) 327 Miles

I woke up around 8am, and was glad to see it had dried up. At least I could pack up in comfort. I had a shower, and then went into the communal kitchen to make some porridge and coffee. Soon I was joined by a couple of Danish women in their sixties. One spoke English well, and chatted with me. They kept laughing every time I answered a question, I wasn't clear if it was my accent or something else, but regardless it made me smile. Compared to me they were like a well-oiled machine, preparing a delicious looking breakfast salad. Next their husbands arrived, and there were exchanges in Danish, followed by further hoots of laughter at my expense.

Finally we were joined by two German bikers, who were in the other tent. They were around my age and were very friendly, asking me about my trip. It was crowded now so I bid my farewell and set off to pack-up.

I had been thinking that my route south was in theory going to take about five to six days, and as this was Sunday that would get me back to the ferry terminal around Thursday or Friday. Currently my ferry was booked for the Sunday. I pondered whether I could take some more of Germany in, or perhaps get an earlier ferry. At that point the earlier ferry seemed preferable, as I felt I had achieved my goal, and now I was simply riding home. I decided to leave it stewing in my head, and take a look at options when I had a wireless connection.

That thought process did however highlight to me how foolishly unprepared I was for the 2000 mile trip back south. I had researched absolutely nothing beyond the route north to Nordkapp. That was a really dumb thing to do, based on the fact I should have been making the most of a good chunk of trip. The other element to add to the process was that when I typed Amsterdam into the Garmin, it showed up as only 1300 miles. I was sure that I had checked Google maps and it was 2000 miles. Maybe I got it wrong, I foolishly convinced myself.

I set off and back tracked down the same road I had travelled last night. As usual it felt a lot quicker going back. This was aided by a good sleep, and less wind. Sea tunnels still bothered me, and I was glad when I saw the glow of daylight ahead. I pulled over for fuel just before rejoining the E6 at Smorfjord. Once again the shop was shut, but the automated pumps were in operation. There was a bunch of about ten BMW's on an organised tour in front of me with German plates. The tour guide was at one pump, and the bikes moved through one at a time as he fuelled them up. I joined the back of the queue and when it was my turn I pushed the bike up to him with the fuel cap open. He looked at me confused, then alarmed, finally breaking into a smile and waving his finger at me.

From there it was a reasonable trip to a town called Lakselv. I thought about having lunch here, but it was a grubby downtrodden place, full of angry looking indigenous teenagers, so I fuelled up the bike rather than my stomach. I was to later learn that this part of the Norway has very high unemployment, leading to lots of unhappiness and crime. You could feel it in the air.

From there the route took me through a military area called Porsangermoen. I noticed a sign for a cafe and pulled in to what looked like an ex military barracks, with several detached bunkhouses and some caravans dotted around. The cafe was in one of the bunk houses. It had character, Wi-Fi and the owner was welcoming. I ordered an omelette which I had craved ever since my last one, just south of the Arctic Circle. I felt relaxed surfing the net, enjoying the excellent omelette and hot coffee. I made another attempt to top up my phone and this time was successful. I searched the DFS Ferry site, established that there was a Friday sailing and took a note of the phone number.

I was in an upbeat mood as I left the cafe and pulled back out onto the main road. A few hundred yards after I pulled out a red pick-up truck zoomed past me, and for some reason I decided to catch up and follow it. I knew I was over the measly 50mph speed limit, but I felt safe behind the truck. I am sure you can guess what's coming next. We came over the brow of a hill and landed right in a Norwegian Police speed trap.

There was one guy with the speed gun and one in a lay by doing the paperwork. The pick-up truck and I were both waved in, behind a couple of motorbikes. Within a few seconds the policeman waved the pick-up on. That troubled me. I took off my helmet and observed the policeman dealing with the bikers. They were Italian, and only one of them was being booked. I compared accessories with the other biker, as we admired each other's GS's. I smiled as the policeman and used a currency converter on his i-phone to deliver the bad news to the extremely animated Italian.

I know it's an old cliché, but the policeman did actually look very young as he finally approached me. He explained very politely that I had been caught doing 95km/h in an 80 km/h zone but as they had a tolerance it was reduced to 92km/h. He advised me that equated to a fine of 2600 Norwegian kroner's.

"Do you want me to convert it to pounds?" he said, with his movie star smile beaming at me.

"Yes please" I said.

It turned out to be ridiculous £275. I mean we're talking 60mph in a 50mph zone on a country road. I was livid.

"So what happened to the pick-up driver?" I asked.

He looked a little troubled and walked over to his speed gun touting mate. He came back and told me that his mate didn't get an accurate reading. I stared at him and shook my head -it didn't stack-up. I mulled it over in my head for a second or two, but decided to cooperate and not push it any further, just in case they were able to come up with some other issues. To this day I wish I had pushed it harder, as I am sure there was something wrong going on. I suspected that it might have been a military guy they let off. Anyway the young cop filled in the paperwork, apologized for the hefty fine, and advised me to wait for a reminder which would then give me an option of paying by installments. We said our goodbyes and I was on my way feeling quite dejected.

Smiley Cop

Unfortunately the dejection coincided with some of the most boring roads I had come across. I finally left the Arctic Highway/Blood road (E6) at the town of Karasjok, and headed inland towards Finland on the 92 which consisted of long straight roads over fairly barren ground at a nut wrenching, bum breaking 50mph. With my mood affecting my physical state, watching the Garmin count down the miles to the next junction was like watching paint dry. I was at my lowest point on the trip.

Eventually I joined the E8 having reached Finland and it was exactly as had been described - straight roads, lots of trees and mosquito's. It was amazing, almost as if the mosquito's all lived just over the border; they swarmed me at any stop. It reminded me of trips to the highlands of Scotland where I have learned to wear my helmet as I pack up my tent on a damp morning to keep the midges away. I began to think about accommodation for the night. The weather was good, but I didn't fancy dealing with the mosquitoes; history has taught me that they have a particular liking for my blood. So it was a choice between a cabin and a hotel.

I had my first Finnish fuel up at Muonio in Lapland, and within a few miles I noticed a sign for a Harriniva hotel to my right. It was early evening so I decided to take a look. I rode up a tree lined avenue and arrived at what looked like a Santa Claus hotel. It was a pine chalet style, and overlooked a lake with a couple of tour buses parked outside.

I parked up and walked towards reception where a tatty old Harley was parked by the door. Inside again was all pine, and had a gift shop selling all sorts of Christmas gear. It was commercial, a bit tacky, but great. I checked for availability and was delighted when the receptionist could give me a room for 90 Euros. Beside me checking in was a snowy haired middle aged guy with Harley gear on. It seemed as though I had just secured the last of the standard rooms, so they could only offer him a room with a sauna at around 130 Euros. He was humming and hawing when I smiled at him and said "you should go for it". He looked at me a little surprised then replied. "Your right I will take it".

I made my way up to my room which was quite a long way as it was a rambling complex of numerous buildings, connected by corridors. The room was a good size, and perfect for the night. I went back to the bike, and moved it beside the old Harley which sat alongside a shiny new one outside of reception. After that I made a couple of trips from bike to room with gear and set about getting my gear organised. I called the Ferry Company and was delighted to hear they could change my ferry booking to the Friday, for a fee of forty pounds. I had feared that the ticket might be non transferable or the ferry full, which made the £40 easy to live with. At last it was time to go find that elusive cold draft beer.

The hotel restaurant was nice, and I saw they had a buffet set up. As I've mentioned I'm not a buffet fan, so I took a seat ordered a cold beer and asked for an a la carte menu. The cold beer was a Finnish brand called Karhu, and was absolutely delightful. Great taste and very refreshing, it had been worth the wait. The Harley guy who had been at reception came in with his wife, and sat at the next table. I ordered a Reindeer stew which came with potatoes and a cranberry sauce.

As I sat there surfing on my i-pad I realized I had forgotten to post the card I had for my daughter Stephanie, in Australia. It had the appropriate Norwegian stamp already affixed. I knew the Harley guy was Norwegian, so I asked them if they would mind posting it for me at the end of their trip. They said they would be delighted to, and asked me to join them at their table. I thanked them and said I would have a beer with them after my dinner which was still to be served.

The Reindeer stew was excellent, and I was feeling nice and relaxed after my second beer. An overweight guy with a short scruffy beard and a pony tail wearing a dark Harley T-shirt joined the Harley couple, and they talked away in animated Norwegian. I assumed he was part of their group. I listened for a while enjoying the sing song tones mixed with much laughter about what, I had no idea. When my plate was cleared I made my move and sat at the one remaining seat at the Harley table, and offered to buy a round of drinks. The newly arrived Harley guy looked concerned, until the Harley couple advised him that I was a biker too. The original Harley guy's name was Svein, the new one was Michael and Svein's wife's name remained 'Svein's wife'.

We instantly connected. The couple were from Trondheim and were big time Harley enthusiasts, being prominent members of their local chapter. They were on a two week tour that would culminate in a rally somewhere back in Norway, or maybe in Sweden, I can't remember. He worked in IT sales, and I got the impression they were well to do and middle class. They were clearly very friendly, having only met the other guy as they parked their bikes.

Michael (the other guy) was a different animal altogether. He was Swedish, but now lived on the far northern Norwegian island of Spitsbergen and worked as a taxi driver. I could tell by looking at him that he had had a full-on life, and that was how it turned out to be. He recounted some of his life stories including a failed marriage that took place in a castle in Scotland (he could not remember which one), a relationship with a lady who was eventually subject to a vicious revenge attack from her ex husband, to his life as a plumber and oil man.

I liked him and observed real humanity in him as we talked about the Spitsbergen polar bear attack that happened the previous year. There had been a failure in the electric wire protecting a camping group of British students that resulted in the tragic death of a seventeen year old. We both reflected on what must have been the horror of the situation.

Mr. and Mrs. Svein and Michael

We continued to order more beers, and it felt good to have some direct human interaction again. Svein's wife started to question his decision to participate in another round, and soon he was ushered to his room. Michael and I sat for another 10 minutes, and then called it a night. I wandered back to my room with my beer buzz, content having had an all-round good night.

Day 11 (Monday) 479 Miles

I felt fine in the morning as I headed down for breakfast. I have a thing where I prefer to breakfast on my own, so I hoped none of the others would be around. As I picked up some bread and cheese, I noticed Svein and his wife, and they said hello. I felt it was a little awkward for them also, but we did the right thing and sat together with not too much interaction. I finished up really quickly, and told them I was off to get the bike packed.

I did the pack horse march between my room and the bike and after three trips I was ready to go. Michael and Svein were out at their bikes by that time, and we discussed the merits of each other's machines. Michael true to form had an old beat-up soft tail Harley, and wore an open face helmet and goggles, whereas Svein had a shiny new Electra Glide equipped with all the goodies.

I was first to go, and waved goodbye as I pulled away. I remember as a younger man being deeply bothered by the fact I would never see people I had connected with again. I guess I have experienced it so many times now that I accept it.

The sun was shining and it was a beautiful day as I headed back out onto the endless straight forest lined roads. After a while I noticed my Sat Nav was playing up again, with the brightness on the screen going down to a barely readable low setting. I pulled over, and as I took a look at it Mr. and Mrs. Svein pulled alongside me to check I was ok. I confirmed I was, and took a final photo of them before they pulled away.

I got the Sat Nav operating again and moved on, experiencing a couple more great encounters with some Reindeer who were wandering along the road, not a care in the world. After a while the Sat Nav directed me to turn right off the E8 onto the 39, and within a few miles I rolled into Sweden. Same straight roads with trees but nevertheless a new country with fewer mosquitoes. The other noticeable difference was the road signs didn't have the 'Russian' feel that the Finnish ones had.

On I rode, focusing on the next goal - the next Sat Nav turn - which indicated 50 miles. Much to my delight, for the first time in a while, the countryside opened up a little and gaps in the forest appeared revealing rolling green pastures.

When I finally reached the turn, I came upon a road that was under reconstruction. As I had found in Norway when they do repairs, they literally just rip the surface off the road, and have you drive over it. This however was on a gigantic scale compared to anything I had seen so far, and lasted for miles. I was really glad to be on the GS, and I was constantly standing on the pegs. It was a pleasure for the first 20 miles or so, but after that it was a bit of a drag.

Having successfully made it through the road works I came past a town of Overkalix, and found a cafe that looked as if it would hit the spot. There was one other older guy sitting in a corner wearing a baseball cap who smiled at me as I walked in. At the counter I was served by a very friendly lady of Asian ethnicity. I ordered the meatballs and a black coffee. You have to order the meat balls in Sweden don't you, to compare them with your local IKEA? She advised me it included a soft drink so I picked a sprite. I realised as I paid that I had no Swedish currency, but she took cards so it wasn't an issue. I decided I would give myself a little challenge, and try riding the length of the country without local currency. When the food came it was delicious. I had that inner contentment of knowing that I had picked just the right place. I pored over my map, and realized I was at the corner where the east coast of Sweden begins, close to the start of the fast road that I had been told about by Willie all those months ago.

Sure enough after a few miles I turned onto the E4 and the speed limit signs indicated a limit of 120kmh/75mph, fantastic on these long and boring roads. More trees, more straights and no view of the sea summed up the rest of the day, as I shifted my bum from one place to the other. It was on that road that I noticed my Sat Nav had re-adjusted itself, and that the distance to Amsterdam was now further than when I had left the Nordkapp. I realised that the Sat Nav has a limited range and will only show a certain amount of distance. As you get closer it then re-sets itself to cover a further part of the route. So I spent the day trying to ride to a point where I was actually within Sat Nav range of Amsterdam. This involved re-setting the route at every coffee, fuel and pee stop. It was a very frustrating process.

I started to make up some games to break the monotony. First I played 'spot the Swedish plated car that is not an estate car', but there were none. I upped the stakes and added in a Volvo Estate car, but there were none. Next it was onto Dutch plated cars without a caravan, and again I was stumped.

It turned out to be my highest mileage propelled by my desire to get to within Sat Nav range of Amsterdam and when I did I was ready for my stop. The weather was good, so I had my heart set on camping. I pulled off at a site just after the town of Ornskolsvik but it was unattractive, so I rode on and entered a National Park area called Skuleskogen.

I was tired, sore and getting a little desperate now, so I started to look for any option including hotels. A sign for Docksta Vandrahem & Camping with food facilities appeared, so I gladly pulled over and entered the site which looked a bit too family orientated for me. Still I was going no further, so I paid at reception, discovered the restaurant was closing and went off to set-up my tent. The site turned out to be fine, and I ended up pitching close to a Swiss biker who was also on his own. He gave me the distinct impression he wanted it to stay that way, so I made no attempt to connect with him. I started cooking my second meatballs meal of the day, this time a Hot n Spicy camping meatball pack that I had brought with me. I had previously sampled them, and knew they were delicious.

As I cooked a young Danish man with albino white hair approached me for a chat. He had a great face full of character. He was cycling around the Baltic Sea and was eager to hear about my trip. He moved on just as my food was ready, and I had a nice end to the evening sitting outside the tent with some red wine and meatballs surveying all around me. There were families cooking dinner, kids playing in the distance and the sound of muffled conversations going on in tents. I felt relaxed with the world.

Bed for the night

I have a habit of lovingly staring at my bike in those situations. I'm sure it's driven by the fact that it's a decent bike. I had the most horrendous unreliable crap bikes as a teenager while my friends who were clearly better at managing their money than me had some seriously good ones. I actually bought my first good bike at the age of 40 and have managed to keep things that way since. Bottom line is I appreciate it.

Day 12 (Tuesday) 468 Miles

The next morning I brewed some coffee, but decided I would stop off somewhere for breakfast, knowing I was facing another mega ride. There was a middle aged English couple in the kitchen where I cleaned my coffee pot. It was strange to hear native English being spoken again. Soon I was packed up and off once again before most other campers had stirred.

I came upon the large town of Sundsvall which had a McDonalds, and decided that would do me nicely. It proved to be the start of a bit of a McDonald's fest. I pulled up beside another fully loaded motorcycle, and after inspecting it, wandered in. The place was empty of customers except the other biker, who was in his twenties and sat eating breakfast in the corner. I ordered my Egg and Bacon McMuffin meal, and noted my sense that being there somehow marked my return to mainstream civilization like the mountain man coming back into town. I asked the biker where he was off to, and it turns out he was Swedish, and a local, just about to set off on a tour of Germany.

I set off again with Stockholm as my minimum goal; it was to be another long mind numbing and bum breaking journey. After a few hundred miles I entered Stockholm, and the route took me right through the city - a bit like the M8 which cuts straight through the centre of Glasgow. On the southern side I hate to admit it, but again I stopped at a McDonalds for a late lunch.

I was tired and it just seemed easy. The sun was shining, so I sat outside, but I could see a storm brewing in the direction I was heading. I observed the Swedes going about their normal life as I sat finishing off my chicken burger. Young Mums herding kids in for food, truck drivers taking a break and shoppers visiting the Electronics store across the road .I pulled out the map again, and noticed a large lake named Vattern, about halfway to Malmo where the bridge crosses to Denmark. I thought that might be a good place to find a hotel.

I pressed on and soon hit a storm. It was fairly heavy rain followed by sunshine, in half hour bursts. I pulled off before my goal of Lake Vattern, when I saw a hotel sign; it turned out to be closed. Boarded up like that, it reminded me of the hotel in the classic horror movie 'The Shining'.

As I pressed on, the storm became more intense and the rain was beating down so hard that it was becoming dangerous. This was no ordinary rain; it was so intense it was actually stinging my lips. The situation was made worse by the fact that my headlight bulb failure warning lamp had come on.

I pulled off the road into a service station, and sheltered under the canopy with a coffee to warm me up, while a middle aged Swedish man came in and fuelled up his Volvo. As he came back from paying I asked him if he was a local and knew of any hotels close by. It turns out he wasn't, but he directed me to the lake Vattern area I had targeted earlier, where he said there were quite a few hotels.

The rain eased, so I moved on with 40 or 50 miles to go to the lake area. Again I was very tired by the time I got there, and I pulled off the road to follow the Garmin's instructions to a hotel. It was a longer diversion that I thought, but when I got there it looked very posh. It was an old building, very classy with oak floors, chandeliers and white linen covered dining tables complete with burning candles. I thought to hell with it, I'll treat myself and have a nice candlelit dinner with some fine wine.

As I walked in squelching wet, I was quickly approached by a young man whom I presumed was the manager. He couldn't wait to tell me he had no vacancies, as he almost pushed me back towards the car park. I guess I didn't realize what a sight I was, dripping water all over his nice wooden floors after a day of storms. I was irritated, but there was nothing else for it but to move on.

I made my way back to the highway, and continued south. I didn't have to go much further before another hotel or in this case, motel, appeared on the Garmin. This time it was just off the highway and faced the lake. It was the Motel Vida Vattern which looked fairly basic, again reminding me of an ex-military building. There was a restaurant and availability, in an ugly chalet that brought back memories of sixties Butlin's holiday camps. Still it was warm and dry, so I happily checked in. I unloaded my wet gear and got my brolly out to make a dash down to the restaurant, which turned out to be more like a cafe.

I picked up some salmon on bread, a beer and sat at a table looking onto the lake. It was good to chill out at last. I then wandered back to my chalet, and sorted out my gear. Between heavy showers I attempted to change the headlight bulb, but couldn't get the clip to re-seat. It was very frustrating and I felt quite ashamed of myself; the big adventure biker couldn't change a light bulb. The new bulb was working, so I did a temporary fix by stuffing gaffer tape behind it to hold it in place. The sky was getting dark and the rain came on again as I finished it off; it was definitely time for bed.

Day 13 (Wednesday) 425 Miles

I woke up in the early hours of the morning with a start: it was pitch dark. I hadn't experienced that for days, and it genuinely took me by surprise. Then I fell back to sleep and woke up again around 7am, with sunshine streaming through the curtains. Great, I thought, a dry start at least. I had a warm shower, which for the first time in a long while did not require coins. I contemplated having another go at the light bulb fitment, but decided against it.

I decided instead to look for a BMW dealer in Copenhagen where I could pick up a t-shirt, have a coffee and talk them into sorting my bulb fitment out. After locating the dealership address in Google, I packed up and headed down for breakfast. It was a new set of staff and I had to go through the process of explaining that breakfast was included in my rate.

I sat there with my bread and cheese, looking out to the vast lake, wondering whether to do the ferry or bridge over to Denmark. Let's just see what the Garmin does, I decided. I filled up the tank at a station next to the motel, and hit the road. It was a fast road with several 120 kph sections. The countryside was again mainly tree lined, flat and a tad boring. The bright sunshine gave way to more torrential showers, and I pulled in to don my waterproof over suit. No matter what I did my boots got wet in the rain. It wasn't because of the rain soaking through, more running down inside. This is clearly the big disadvantage of short boots, and it was something I needed to address for my next trip.

As I rode on I noticed an airplane that had been converted to a cafe on my right hand side which raised a smile. Had I known it was coming up, I would have sampled its cuisine. Further down the road I stopped off for fuel and a coffee, and noticed a Swedish tourist shop which presented another chance to pick up some gifts. Not of great quality I must add, but it's the thought that counts. I wandered around amongst the tack finally settling on some stickers, magnets and a t-shirt.

Swedish Moose Sticker

It was at that point that I suddenly thought I had left my visa card at the garage beside last night's motel. I started emptying my pockets and rummaging through my luggage in desperation. I even went to the length of calling the garage before I eventually found it in another section of my wallet. Panic over.

Eventually I made it to Malmo, a place I had spent a little time in years gone by with work, so it was a thrill to ride past it. Clearly the Garmin had opted for the bridge, as it loomed just beyond Malmo. I hate tolls especially when I have no local cash, but the process was very easy with clearly marked credit card signs. A lady appeared out of nowhere to deal with the fact I was a bike, and not paying a car rate. Swedish efficiency indeed.

I had done it. I had ridden the length of Sweden and spent two nights without any cash. Here's to technology I whispered to myself. The crossing was great as it was sunny again, and the engineering was to be marveled at comprising of a massive sea bridge followed by a trip over some islands, then finally a tunnel emerging in Copenhagen, Denmark by the Airport. The exit was right beside the Hilton where Amber and I had stayed earlier that year on a weekend break. We could have seen me from our room window, I thought to myself.

I continued to follow the instructions on my Garmin, looking forward to arriving at the Copenhagen BMW bike dealership. After one missed turn I soon arrived at my destination, but there was no sign of the dealership. I went up and down the street but there was nothing even resembling a bike shop.

I pulled into a nearby petrol station and asked inside. The guy pointed at a tall building and said it's a headquarters, not a shop. Damn it I cursed to myself, I should have checked my Google find more thoroughly. The guy was trying to be helpful, and directed me to a street where he said I would find BMW, Audi etc. "Bikes also?" I asked, He shrugged his shoulders, but said "of course".

I was unconvinced as I sat on the kerb, contemplating my next move. I had to strip off the bike gear, as the pouring rain had changed to hot sun. I decided to move on and out of Copenhagen.

As I crossed the countryside a plan emerged in my head. I could ride to the hotel where I had originally stayed in Denmark, as I knew it was of good quality and had good food. I could then take two days instead of one to get back to the ferry and call in at a German BMW dealer. I typed it into my Garmin and saw that I had around 150 miles to go. I was sorted.

I expected a tunnel between Copenhagen and Odense but it was another massive sea bridge. As I approached it the weather was dry, but the clouds ahead looked a bit grim. I paid the toll and proceeded onto the bridge. As I left dry land I could feel the wind buffeting me quite strongly. The bridge at 1.6km has the world's third longest main span and is very impressive. It makes the Forth Road or Golden Gate bridges seem quite tame by comparison.

As I started to climb towards the apex of the bridge I saw a storm rolling towards me. It reminded me of something you might see in one of the mid-western states of America. When it hit me it was the same torrential rain I had experienced earlier, along with severe gusts of wind. I was instantly soaked and was buffeted from side to side. I wasn't sure how to deal with it, but dropping a couple of gears and continuing at a pace of about 50mph seemed to help. I was on edge as I shifted my body weight with the wind, and held the handlebars tightly. Just over the apex there was a gust of wind that caught me from one side, then the other, had me zigzagging in the lane. It was a great relief to get back down and into calmer air. It was not just the thought of falling off that was scary, but the possibility of being blown into the low barrier and ending up in the sea; that was a real nightmare scenario.

Soon after I left the bridge I noticed a huge build up of traffic on the other side of the highway and wondered if they had actually closed the bridge due to the wind. I carried on, a little anxious in the knowledge that there was a further sea crossing to go. I hope it's a tunnel I thought to myself, as the rain continued to soak me and make riding miserable.

When I did finally approach the crossing I saw the towers of another bridge looming ominously at me in the distance. I pulled off at a service station just before and had a relaxing coffee and ice cream. Then I made sure the sky was clear before setting off.

I took a deep breath as I headed onto the bridge waiting for the wind battering that never came to be. Thankfully it was a shorter and lower crossing, and the wind, whilst fairly strong, was at a very manageable level. From there on I was on mainland Europe, and soon reached the exit for my hotel on the A7. I pulled into the familiar petrol station and filled up for my journey tomorrow. I also picked up a couple of glass size red wines as a relaxation aid for later in the evening.

After around a seven mile ride I approached the familiar and welcome site of Hotel Kløver. The same receptionist with dyed bright red hair checked me into the same room one as before. I unpacked my gear and laid out various pieces of wet clothing across radiators to dry. I had a warm and vey welcome shower, which felt fantastic after the day's long and wet ride. It was still raining outside, so the alfresco dining plan that I had in my head was not going to happen. I asked the red haired girl if I could have a table, and she seated me in what I thought was a busy dining room for a Wednesday evening. Mind you I could understand why as the food, ambience and the service had been excellent last time around. The poor red headed girl seemed to be playing a lot of roles as she took my order for a cold beer and the T-bone steak special (medium rare).

After diner I wandered contentedly back to my room and checked out Hamburg BMW dealers, of which there were two, then settled for the night.

Day 14 (Thursday) 327 Miles

I woke to hear the rain battering my window, and was again taken by surprise at the darkness. I find it amazing how quickly the human mind becomes accustomed to a certain way of being. I decided to leave the bike packing process until the last minute, hoping the rain would subside.

I took the short walk to the breakfast room, which I hadn't experienced last time due to my early start. There was a couple in their thirties sitting at a table. It was very noticeable that there was little communication between them. It felt like an uncomfortable silence. Maybe it was my imagination but an air of unhappiness seemed to hang over them like a cloud.

I finished off my breakfast and made my way back to my room, noticing on the way that sun had come out. I had already done some packing the night before, so it was simply a case of loading the bike. The bike was soaked from what had been heavy overnight rain, and I wiped away the puddles from the seat with my hand. I had another needle in a haystack check for the earplug I had dropped in the gravel first time around, with no success.

I wandered back in to set-up the Garmin with the addresses of the Hamburg BMW dealers I had identified last night. It felt good that I had a plan, despite not being clear exactly where I would stay that night. I opened the I-Pad to pull off the dealership addresses only to find the wireless connection was not working.

I walked along to reception to get it sorted, but was told the man with the skills would not arrive until 10am; it was before 8am at that point. I told them it probably just needs a modem reboot, but the lady stood her ground and repeated 10am. Damn it I thought to myself, why didn't I take care of this last night. I didn't want to hang around, so decided to press on and get wireless somewhere on the way. I had noticed that there was a McDonalds located just before I would re-join the highway, which would do the trick.

I paid the bill and took a final look at Hotel Kløver as I pulled away. The roads were still wet, but the sun was shining. It was about a seven mile ride to McDonalds, where I pulled in and parked up. There was a group of teenagers congregated by some cars as if at the start of some organised day trip. I walked up to the entrance only to find it was closed and didn't open until 10am. Is there another McDonalds on the planet earth that doesn't open until 10am, I fumed to myself.

I remounted the bike and pulled off onto the highway. I fumed for a little longer then concluded that I would just have to find somewhere else. I had the Garmin set to locate food places as I entered Germany, and before long a McCafe showed up on the screen. Hmmm I thought to myself this sounds like a young entrepreneur taking the piss out of McDonalds. Surely they will have Wi-Fi.

I pulled off and rode the 5 miles or so to find it. When I did find it I was disappointed to find McCafe was a brand of Coffee Shop, located inside a McDonalds. Still it was open, and it must have Wi-Fi. The first member of staff spoke no English; pointing and waving and speaking in a German accent was not working for me, so she called over a lady with some English. She nodded and handed me an instruction leaflet in German. Game on, I said to myself as I started to locate the Wi-Fi. After some messing about I determined I was in fact snookered, as you had to have a German mobile number to operate it. I felt very frustrated as I set off again towards the Autobahn.

"OK, think", I muttered to myself "how do I solve this?" I mulled it over as I rode back through the town, looking for any obvious signs of places that might offer Wi-Fi. I passed a hotel on the other side of the road, just before reaching the Autobahn, and considered going into the car park to see if I could catch their hopefully unsecured signal. Too late now, I thought as hit the main route to Hamburg again. Suddenly a light came on in my head, I had a possible solution. I would set my mobile to roaming, and as quickly as possible locate the addresses and get them into my Garmin.

I excitedly awaited the next service station, where I pulled in to execute my plan. I couldn't see why it wouldn't work, but I was still a little apprehensive based on earlier events. Within minutes I had executed my plan, and not only did I have the address but the first one I had located was only a mile or so off my route through Hamburg.

I was buzzing with excitement as I pulled back onto the highway and accelerated hard to get to autobahn pace. I suddenly heard an unusual clunking noise, and looked down only to discover that my Sat Nav had fallen off its mount, and was somewhere behind me on the highway. I was absolutely gutted, stunned in a way that shut me down. I was in a trance like state as I continued along the road. I knew it was a defense mechanism, so I happily stayed with it.

After ten minutes or so I went through a very slow and logical thought process. Is it worth turning back I queried, considering it would be a least a twenty mile round trip and the chances of safely finding my Garmin in a working state would be more than slim. It's not so bad I ruminated, I mean its only my £450 Garmin that was going to lead me not only to the dealership, but also to accommodation for tonight, then the ferry port tomorrow. I was gutted and just to add to the mood the heavy rain returned.

I pulled off at the next service station, and contemplated my options. I checked out a map in a shop noting down the major towns on the way. I decided that I at least needed to get beyond Hamburg and then think about a hotel. I remembered my outward journey as I entered Hamburg, feeling relatively at ease with my directions as I made my way past the city. I looked beyond the highway, imagining that gleaming dealership with hot coffee and great t-shirts just waiting to be bought.

As I left Hamburg I started towards Bremen, which was straight forward. Then it was Oldenburg, where it got complicated. When I finally reached Oldenburg I was looking for signs for Groningen in the Netherlands, and was reminded that mainland European states are not too good at advertising neighboring countries cities in their road signs.

At one point in the pouring rain I was totally unclear whether I was on the right road or not, so I pulled off into an unknown town. I sat there looking for someone to ask directions, but there was no-one around. Frustrated, I made my way back towards the highway, and just before the "which way "decision needed to be made, a young mum pulled up beside me at the lights in a Golf. I ushered her to roll down the window and shouted "Which way to

Groningen?" She smiled and pointed right. I smiled and gratefully gave her the thumbs up.

I headed back onto the highway and sure enough after a few miles a sign for Groningen appeared. My next task was to find accommodation. As I raced towards the Dutch border, I noticed what looked like a big electronics store to my right where there was also fuel and food, and pulled in. I decided to fill up the bike first and then myself with Kentucky Fried Chicken.

This was followed by a visit to the electronic store in search of a Sat Nav. The store was large and bright, full of all sorts of gizmos. I asked a young guy if they did Sat Nav; he said yes, and led me to the display. I explained my situation and he excitedly showed me a Garmin Motorcycle Sat Nav, unfortunately not my model. I checked the connection to see if it was the same as my bike mount, sadly it was not, so I thanked him and moved on.

I re-joined the highway and continued towards the Netherlands. This border territory didn't look like a great place to stay, so I decided I would continue across the border. I stopped off for fuel just over the border, and asked the attendant about the route and hotels. He enthusiastically got a map out, and showed me some options. I should continue through Groningen then on to a junction where there were two alternative routes towards Amsterdam. One was the impressive route across the Afsluitdijk that I had used on my way up, and the other took a more southerly route. I also asked him about accommodation, but he had no great suggestions on offer.

I continued on and passed through Groningen, which was busy with traffic, thankfully only on the opposite side from me. I then continued along the highway observing a camper van with a motorcycle loaded on a rear rack. I quite fancy that I thought to myself. Eventually I approached the junction where the two alternative routes to Amsterdam were. I didn't need to decide tonight I concluded, as I spotted a hotel sitting just off the junction. I would stay there for the night.

It was called the Hage Hotel Joure, located in Rijksweg on the edge of Friesland, where the black and white cows hail from. The price was 80 Euros, which seemed reasonable. The rate didn't include breakfast but, more importantly, it did include Wi-Fi. The room was at the back of the hotel and was clean and spacious in the American style, certainly the best hotel room I had experienced on the trip.

I brought my bike around to the back of the hotel, and parked it just outside my door. There was an un-alarmed fire escape door out to the bike, which made the unpacking process easy. After that I wandered along to the restaurant where I ate poor tasting fish and chips, served by a grumpy Dutch woman before retiring with a beer to my room.

Ok, I said to myself, shit happens and you have to get this trip back on song. "I said I would visit a BMW dealer and I will visit a BMW dealer", I announced out loud to the hotel room mirror. Robert the Bruce did not give up and neither will I. I connected to Wi-Fi and located Harry Meijer's BMW dealership, which was located just off my route to the ferry. I had decided to take the southern route, and wrote out instructions via Google Maps on a piece of paper. Who needs Sat Nav, I thought as I climbed into bed for my last night's sleep on continental Europe for this trip.

Day 15 (Friday) 127 Miles

The final day in continental Europe was a wet one as I woke from my sleep, which had been disturbed by one or more mosquitoes in my room. I have painful memories of hearing the same sound buzzing around my head on a bike tour in Greece in 2005 resulting in some very sore bites in the morning. I hid under the covers, but it was very warm and uncomfortable. Then I had a brainwave, I would put my midge head net on, then I would be protected. So at around 2am I flapped about feeling for the lamp switch, resulting in me knocking the lamp over, followed by my untouched glass of sweet sticky Drambuie dribbling onto the bed sheets. In the end I couldn't find my midge net, and ended up moving to the other bed, which was clean and falling back to sleep.

When I woke there was no sign of additional bites, which was a relief. I expect the mosquitoes focused in on the spilled Drambuie and were suffering the consequences.

I got things organised in a slow fashion, recognizing that I was in no hurry. I took the disc lock off the bike, to make sure I had no lapse of memory later on. I had a close shave experience in the highlands with a lock on my wheel, which I failed to remove prior to setting off. The result was that it had inadvertently loosened a nut that allowed brake fluid to escape. I remember pulling on the front brake to turn into Eilian Donan castle with no effect. Luckily there was nothing in front so it was a lucky escape.

I wandered over to McDonalds for breakfast. I was a bit sick of McDonalds, but 5 Euros made it more attractive than 11 Euros in the hotel. That's 6 Euros towards my Garmin.

On my return to the room I spotted my friend Raymond on Skype, and talked briefly as he was still at work in Australia. After that I finished packing the bike. A coat hanger kept the Fire Exit door open for me as I moved between the room and the bike.

I settled the bill and walked out into the rain, Amsterdam bound. I stuck the directions that I had created the night before on my screen with duck tape, and I was off. The rain was persistent but not the crazy heavy stuff I had been experiencing, just plain old constant rain. I got onto the A6, recognising that I had a about 60 miles to go before the first of a few turns. The roads were relatively quiet and moving quickly. Around the 60 mile mark I saw my junction and followed it, pulling off soon after for fuel. I confirmed with a guy in the garage that I was on the right route. He shouted "A9 all the way".

Not long after I moved off I saw a sign for Schipol/Utrecht A9, which was what was stuck to my windscreen. I thought for a few seconds, picturing the map in my mind, and decided to go for it. Also further down my instructions dictated I was to leave the A9 at exit 7.

I continued to follow the signs for Schipol, then started counting the junctions up. I was very pleased with myself, and found not having a Garmin telling me the status of everything quite freeing. After junction 6 I was poised for my exit when the road split, two lanes on each side. One was the continuation of the A9 and the other Schipol. Is this junction seven I wondered? My instincts said no, and I continued on; junction seven appeared shortly after. How can a junction not be a junction, I wondered, but was not that bothered: I was nearly there.

I made the last few turns, and was where I expected Harry Meijer's BMW to be, but it wasn't. I stopped and asked a guy at a small garage, and he pointed to a building a street away. As I rode into the dealership I thought to myself, you can take my Garmin but you can't take away my freedom!

The dealership was a shiny modern building, with two floors filled with bikes and accessories. I had a good look at the clothing, and picked up a couple of t-shirts. As the lady wrapped them I asked to speak to the service manager. I explained my problem with the headlight bulb, and he said the fitting is most likely broken, recognising it as a common fault.

"That's great", I said, to his surprise, remembering how ashamed of myself I had been when I could not fit it. We went outside and he confirmed his suspicion. He called over a young mechanic who was a typical cocky but charismatic Dutchman.

He said "I can fix this", with a smile and proceeded to take things apart, leaning over my bike with a lit cigarette hanging from his mouth. "A replacement part is about 300 Euros" he said "don't be rushing to change it".

Within 5 minutes he had it up and running again and I thanked him. I went into see the service manager, and he waived away any attempt to pay. "Enjoy your trip home" he said with a smile. I was very grateful for their help and friendly attitude.

I pulled out of the dealers, back into the rain, and headed for the A9 and the signs for Ijmuiden. It was all very straightforward, and I even started to see ferry signs. Before long I was on a street I recognised, running alongside the harbour. Within minutes I was pulling into the street leading down to the ferry. I spotted a cafe on the right hand side, which I decided would be a good option. It was just after 12 noon and check in didn't open until 4pm.

I rode down and saw the ship docked, but there was no-one around, so I turned around and parked up outside the cafe. It was large, but fairly empty as I took my seat. I ordered the Ham and Cheese omelette with frites, which turned out to be ham, two fried eggs and melted cheese slices on top. I understand why the Netherlands is not famous for its cuisine. Still it satisfied my appetite, and gave me shelter from the storm. I extended the shelter with a second coffee, then a sprite as more ferry bound bikers started to appear. I could hear Scottish accents for the first time in a while, and enjoyed observing and listening to the banter (playful chat) between them.

The rain stopped and the sun came out, so I paid up and headed outside to look at the bikes. There was a good variety, everything from a new Triumph Thunderbird Cruiser to an old BMW tourer. Other bikers started to spill out into the sunshine, and soon we were exchanging some details of our trips. I was proud to be the only one to have headed North, and by far having achieved the highest mileage, but it was met with an air of what I can only describe as surprise. Not surprise in a good way, more like why you would do that on your own? What's wrong with you?!

Pre boarding hang out

There was a friendly looking guy in cruiser looking gear and I asked him if the Thunderbird was his. "No" he said "mine is over there", and he pointed to a lovely soft tail Harley. He was from Dumfries, and had been down to Germany with wife in tow. I smiled as he told me he had been directed to a biker pub by some guy in an autobahn service station and had then stayed there for three days. He was a truck driver with a passion for Harleys, and I liked him. The rest of the Scottish bikers were a group from near Dalkeith and were a mixture of middle aged couples and one single rider. Soon it was time to head for the ferry.

We all rode the few hundred yards and joined the queue. As usual I wandered the along the line of bikes (much shorter than the outbound route), and chatted to a couple of them. The Scottish Mafia was now formed in our queue, and arrangements were being made to meet in the bar. I was a bit of "and you too" addition after some inside joke about my Reindeer skin, which I concluded was related to lonely man needing furry company. I felt a little bit irritated by them, feeling they were judging me by their mainstream standard way of living there lives. Maybe I was feeling a little over sensitive.

As we boarded I ended up behind the Harley couple in a very tight space. We helped each other get organised, then I headed up on deck. The cabin number was 911 and it was Friday the 13th of July so all the omens were good. I booked my steakhouse meal and got myself organised. The meal was good, and I enjoyed listening to and observing a Dutch family preparing for their UK holiday. Mum and Dad were telling the kids about all the exciting fun that lay ahead over the next two weeks.

After that it was back to the cabin to do some journal writing. As I was doing that they announced in English, French and Dutch that there were still tickets available for the Muppets movie, which made me smile.

The bike boarded and homeward bound

I had noticed a massage treatment advertised, and wandered off to check it out. A blonde middle-aged Dutch woman was sitting looking bored in her designated area. I asked her if she had availability and she smiled, looking relieved to have a customer, and told me I had to pay in the gift shop. I ordered the neck and back massage, which I think was supposed to be for fifteen minutes, but lasted for at least thirty. It was a relaxing way to spend my last night of the trip.

Day 16 (Saturday) 178 Miles

I had a blissful noise free sleep, and woke up to the announcement that breakfast was now being served. I made my way to the coffee shop and ordered a coffee and pastry, which was delicious. On my way back to my cabin I met the Harley couple, sitting sipping coffee at a seat by the window. I sat down and chatted to them for ten minutes. They told me how they had met up with the other riders, but ended up leaving quite early.

I wandered outside, and observed our arrival at North Shields on what was a cloudy, but dry day. I had another route dilemma. I had a vision of stopping off at my parents as part of the final conclusion to the trip, but had misjudged the arrival time thinking it was 9:30am not 10:30am. When they finally called us down to the bike deck it became obvious we would be even later than 10:30am. The vehicle deck was cramped and hot as we prepared to disembark. Finally the nose of the ship dropped, and we were off. By that time it was after 11am, and I had decided to head straight home, this time up the East coast.

I had never taken this route before; I enjoyed it and cheered as I crossed the border into Scotland. Not much further on I pulled into a busy little establishment named the Cedar Cafe for a full Scottish Breakfast and a hot mug of coffee. It was a novelty to be home again as I observed all around me. Kid's football teams, workers, couples and singles all stopping off for a break.

I continued up the east coast, finally skirting Edinburgh where I stopped for my final fuel stop. Before long I was on the familiar route from Edinburgh to home, and after a further 45 minutes or so pulled into Lenzie.

I felt like the conquering hero as I turned into my street and honked my horn raising my hand as I passed Willie's house. A few hundred feet further on I was home, and as I backed the bike down the driveway Amber came out to greet me. I had done it. I rode to the Nordkapp. With my milometer showing 16,237 miles my total trip mileage had been 5,004 in 16 days. It was the end of an epic trip.

After thoughts

Was it worth it? Absolutely it was an experience of a lifetime. Would I do it again? Yes, but I would change my route home. Now that I made the extreme goals like A and the Nordkapp, I would likely take a more relaxed, less mile burning approach. What would I have done differently? Not much actually. My main error was the lack of research on the route home. Others include taking a warmer sleeping bag, regular waterproof motorcycle boots, carry a spare bike key and don't buy your wife Reindeer socks as a gift. I later found the Reindeer socks in a bag destined for charity. I rescued them off-course.

For me this proves that there is no need to take an all or nothing approach to Adventure Motorcycle riding. While I admire the guys who do the big trips, and yes I would love to do one, there are adventures to found nearer home, do-able within a couple weeks or days. For many it's a testing adventure to take off on their own regardless of the destination. I thoroughly enjoyed my adventure and, as I have read many times, I actually found the challenges thrown at me made the trip better, not worse.

The other thing you read in the long distance travel books is the chance encounters you have with others. Spending a night with Svein, Michael and Mrs. Svein may not equal a night with a desert tribesman, but is was spontaneous, interesting and fun.

What surprised me? The stunning scenery in Norway surpassed my expectations, the lack of interest or interaction from many other bikers and the sheer bloody distance from the Nordkapp to Amsterdam on the route home.

What was my best moment? It had to be that idyllic night at Kovatn camping, with my tent pitched right on the edge of a Fiord facing snow-capped mountains. I sat there on my camping chair in the evening sunshine smoking a cigar, sipping red wine with my bike by my side. It doesn't get much better.

If you have read this book it's likely you are seeking your own adventure, and if that's the case I urge you to do it. Whether it's an overnight camp on your own, or a longer trip, just make the time and take the effort, it will be worthwhile.

Now how far is it to Morocco?

Major Equipment List

BMW R1200GS (2009) – Never missed a beat other than a blown dipped headlight bulb.

Shark Evoline Helmet – Love the helmet but the flip mechanism jammed and left me open face for much of the trip. I have to say though on my return Shark repaired it free of charge via the very helpful staff at Firecrest Motorcycle Outfitters in Glasgow. That's what I call service.

Hein Gericke Two Piece Gortex Suit, One piece rain suit and short boots – The Gortex suit performed well but you really did need the rain suit in the extremely wet conditions. I love the boots for comfort but sadly the rain ran down my trousers into them rendering them useless for wet weather riding.

Colman Phad X2 Tent – Excellent tent, easy to erect after reading the instructions. Proved to be wind and waterproof in some nasty conditions.

Vango Nitstar 350 Sleeping Bag – Generaly good although I had one cold night where the temperature dropped quite low.

Thermorest Sleeping Matt – Excellent piece of kit that is far more comfortable than it looks.

Primus Gravity II Stove – Amazingly powerful compared to the old stoves I have used in the past.

Regatta Deluxe Folding Camping Chair – Very comfortable and a must have item

GSI Outdoors Java – This is a cracking little Coffee kit including a cafetiere and cup which made mornings special

Garmin Zumo 660 Motorcycle Satellite Navigation – Very useful but I did experience issues with an intermittent loss of brightness. I would always carry a Sat Nav but I might be tempted to rely on it less.

Scala Rider G4 Helmet Intercom – Not used at all. Brought it so I would have on bike phone connectivity but in the end it remained switched off for most of the time.

Airhawke Seat Cushion – I could never have done such high mileage without it.